THE COLLEGE ESSAY GUIDEBOOK

Writing a Powerful Story about Yourself

DAVID MANDLER, PH.D.

THE COLLEGE ESSAY GUIDEBOOK

Writing a Powerful Story

about Yourself

DAVID MANDLER PH.D.

New York

Published by Ergo Sum Press
Church Street Station
PO Box 1838
New York, NY, 10008
www.ergo-sumpress.com

Edited by Maya J. Lo Bello
Cover Design by Ágnes Faragó
Back Cover Photo by Julia Lee

ISBN Number: 978-0-9993919-0-7
Library of Congress Control Number: 2017914368

Printed in the United States of America

For my truly awesome children,
Rachel and Benny, with love

Contents

Acknowledgements

It would be a gross act of ingratitude if I did not publicly express my deepest sense of appreciation to my former students, Alex, Andrew, Courtney, Enver, Jannie, Jennifer, Karol, Kyler, Larissa, Laszlo, Namra, and Vandana for their valuable contributions to this book. I am grateful to each one of them for allowing me to make use of their work.

I would like to express my gratitude to a number of people whose observations had an impact not only on the book's content, but also its physical appearance. Eric Grossman's astute observations regarding the manuscript sent me in the right direction. Maya J. Lo Bello's careful edits greatly improved the phrasing and overall coherence of the manuscript. Ágnes Faragó's artistry found ample expression in the cover design while Erzsi Jeges' typesetting skills shaped the interior appearance of the book.

While the actual writing of a book is a solitary activity, like flowers in need of water and sunlight, the right conditions are necessary for a book to be born. Most of this book came into being at my parents' welcoming apartment in Florida during the summer of 2017. I am grateful to my parents, George and Judith, for taking such good care of me in the five-week absence of my wife and children. Their loving support provided the necessary sunshine for this book to blossom. My children, Rachel and Benny, deserve to be acknowledged as the most understanding six- and seven-year-olds ever for letting their Papa spend time revising the manuscript. Last but certainly not least, I'd like to extend my gratitude and appreciation to my wife, Evelyn, for her encouraging words and support over the course of this project.

Preface

Towards the end of September, I asked my high school seniors to record a vivid dream of theirs in detail and offer a Freudian interpretation of it. (We had just finished reading Freud's *Interpretation of Dreams*). The results were quite remarkable. One student dreamed of a magical school bus that turned into a sinking submarine. Another one described a weird interview with a handsome middle-aged man dressed in Navy attire who asked her to cook him a Mexican pilaf (don't ask). A third one found himself aboard a sinking pirate ship, only to end up seconds later in a paradise on earth, which then morphed into a Chelsea soccer game including 44,000 people screaming around him as he fumbled to use a very inadequate camera that he could not control at all. A fourth student described taking an elevator with three other men, two of whom got out on the second floor while the third one, a tall person with a menacing mustache, followed him to his apartment, at which point he was jolted out of sleep. A fifth student found himself in the cafeteria with the lunch lady who, instead of inquiring after his menu choice, began asking Common App essay questions in rapid succession. These are but some of the feverish dreams my otherwise cool, calm, and collected students elected to share with me.

What astonished me the most, though, was the interpretation section of the exercise. Apparently, there was a common cause underlying each dream: the demands and uncertainties associated with the college application process. Accordingly, these anxiety dreams were the products of people living in the type of stress caused by the college application season and all the demands college admission entails.

Reading dozens of similar dream analysis responses gave me the impetus to take action. So, one morning in October, I told my anxious students that, instead of reading great works of literature, we would watch an entire season of *Sponge Bob Square Pants* during the coming school year. All right, I did no such thing, I confess. Doing so would have given *me* anxiety dreams (not to mention an unsolicited trip to the principal's, and later, to the unemployment office). Barring that alternative, I settled upon the next best thing: writing a practical book about the college essay, the results of which are now in front of you. The ultimate aim of this guide is to reduce the unnecessary stress you, the reader, experience during these months in your (rising) senior year.

It is my hope that the sequence of writing discoveries, the terrific advice from my former students and the brief, but relevant grammar review that I have compiled in this book shall provide you with the necessary steps, guidance and confidence to look into yourself, discover something unique about your personality and successfully transform this experience into a fascinating narrative about yourself. If you relax, research, reminisce and revise your writing, you may even come to enjoy this journey. Don't lose sight of the fact that at the end of the road, you will graduate high school and commit to a college that has accepted you.

During the next month, set apart about half an hour to an hour every day strictly for the sake of spending time just with yourself. Each Writing Discovery is intended to help you advance on the path towards self-aware-ness while also enabling you to become more comfortable as a writer. Using all the great material you have produced about yourself in the course of your daily self-explorations will then allow you to fill out your college apps. If you stick to your schedule, by the end of this book you will have acquired some very important writing skills that you can later utilize in crafting papers and essays for your college classes. The first step to this, however, is preparing a very solid college essay and supplements.

Lately, many good advice books have been published about the col-lege essay. This one differs in that I'll stay out of your way as much as I can and give you *something concrete* to do on a regular basis. Instead of spending hours reading *about* how to write the college essay, you will be doing it one small step at a time. You may find that some of the steps are very easy for you while others require more deliberation. That's only to be expected since you are not the only reader of this book (or at least, I sure hope so). Remember: you are in charge of how fast or how slowly you want to progress through the sequence of writing activities. However you decide to proceed, be sure to make each Writing Discovery step count. Doing so may completely eliminate the kind of unproductive stress my students identified as the underlying cause of their anxiety-fueled nightmares.

Introduction

If you are feeling anxious to have the college application process behind you, I have some good news for you: it will be over in just a few months. The even better news is that when it is all over, you *will* have gotten into a college and moved on with your life. The less positive news is that you will have to do a lot of work in the interim with absolutely no guarantee that you will actually end up attending the university you have designated as your dream school. Still, the fact that you are reading this introduction is encouraging; it means that you'd like to find a way to explore who you are as a person and write a genuine, emotionally engaging story about yourself that allows the admissions officers to fall in love with you.

As you may know, Ivy League schools and other (highly) selective colleges are in increasing demand. In the last fifteen years, acceptance rates to Stanford University, for example, have fallen from 15.5 per cent for the class of 2001 to just 4.7 per cent for the class of 2017. The situation is not much better for Harvard. There, acceptance rates have fallen from 12.3 per cent for the class of 2001 to 5.3 percent for the class of 2021. [1] This means that, out of 39,506 applicants to Harvard, just 2,056 were accepted. [2] Across the board, the acceptance rates to Ivy League schools hover between 5 to 15 percent while other selective schools such as Williams, Amherst, Swarthmore, or Middlebury College accepted around 12-16 percent of applicants. The acceptance rates for New York University, Boston University, and Northeastern University mirrored those of CUNY's Baruch College at 27 percent and selective programs such as CUNY's Macaulay Honors at 29 percent.

Because admissions decisions are based on many factors, this process follows a holistic approach. This means that your entire application is scru-

---

[1]   http://www.businessinsider.com/how-hard-to-get-into-harvard-stanford-2017-4
[2]   http://www.thecrimson.com/article/2017/3/31/harvard-regular-admissions-2017/

tinized, from your grades or extracurricular activities to various supplements and writing examples like the Common App or school-specific essay. It's no secret that your GPA weighs in heavily. After all, what are parents for if not to remind you of this bitter fact of life at least once a day while yelling at you to work harder? Extracurricular activities, summer internships, or summer camp work experience also has a place in the application.

With three years of high school behind you, the facts in your application look impressive enough. But now, as the realization hits that it is time to write the personal essays required by the selective, higher educational institutions like those mentioned in the previous paragraph, you may begin to worry that this crucial piece of writing will be the weakest link in your otherwise strong, academic chainmail. You start to think that the personal essay (as well as the supplements) will be the most important pieces you have ever written in high school. And, in a strictly utilitarian sense, this may actually be true.

Still, it bears repeating (before your distress level hits the dial marked *totally-flipped out*) that admissions committees review your *entire file*, of which the personal essay is only *one* piece. Nonetheless, you are not wrong in thinking that this particular assignment is pretty high stakes. As a result, you really need to produce a writing piece that is as carefully polished and genuine as possible.

As is the case for everything you write, you need to keep in mind not only the purpose of the college essay, but also the audience for whom it is written. The purpose of the essay is to capture an essential piece of your personality in an engaging, lively and stimulating way. What about the audience? According to a 2011 survey of the National Association of College Admissions Counseling (NACAC), women make up 70 percent of admissions counseling and assistant/associate director positions at the admissions office. Most women at the admissions office are white and under 40 years of age. [3] When I asked my students to describe the audience,

---

[3]   You can find out much more about the fascinating statistics of the admissions officer here: https://www.nacacnet.org/globalassets/documents/publications/research/careerpaths2014.pdf

that is, the admissions officers who would read their essays, most of them looked baffled. You see, they had never given it a thought. A few moments later, the overwhelming majority of the class spoke of older white men in suits. You can imagine how shocked many of my students were when a flesh-and-blood admissions officer, a woman in her early 30s, walked in moments later, telling my classes that almost everyone in the admissions office where she worked was a woman in her 30s or early 40s. The above-cited survey seems to confirm her experience.

Why does any of this matter? Without sinking into a morass of sexist assumptions, I'll simply rephrase what the aforementioned admissions officer stressed to my class during her visit: the story you choose to detail should be served on an attractive dish that *invites emotional engagement* because women like to be emotionally engaged by a story. Emotionally engaging stories—not to be confused with sob stories or emotionally manipulative ones—tend to make your reader develop sympathy for you and your quest. In other words, they allow for the admissions officer to love something about you and even root for you. Be that as it may, I'll let you in on another secret: men also like to be emotionally engaged by stories. So, in the final analysis, your writing will resonate much more with the reader, no matter his or her gender, if you allow an emotional component to animate it.

How can you get there? First of all, by engaging in much self-reflection, brainstorming and many false starts. Once you have written a few different stories and produced a succession of drafts seen and commented upon by various people whose opinion you trust, you will have created an essay showcasing an experience that illustrates your internal world while demonstrating a significant development in beliefs or change in attitude presented in an emotionally engaging and intellectually exciting way.

One of my very clever students (yes, I only have very clever students) anonymously suggested on the college essay feedback form given at the end of the year that my advice to you should simply be to pull a story out of thin air since the admissions people don't really know if you're writing the truth about yourself or not. It's certainly true that the admissions officers reading your essay will have no idea whether or not the story you present in your essay ever happened. This strategy, though, will only work if you have the ability to create entire worlds populated by three-dimensional characters out of thin air. Most high school seniors (or college seniors, for that matter) need a lot of practice before they can write that way. In addition, there is an ethical dimension to the question. Even if I were equipped to write a completely fictitious story about my struggles with cancer or the death of a close family member, what would submitting a piece like this say about me as a person? Considering the fact that you will very likely elicit feedback from people you trust who know you, let's agree that this route is entirely unacceptable.

Luckily, besides the practical and ethical questions, it's actually easier to recall events and reflect about yourself in writing than fabricate a believable false self. Even the anonymous student—whom, just for the record, I instantly recognized by his self-assured tone and word choices—did not follow his own suggestion. His college essay was about witnessing the sudden death of his father as a child and his reaction to it (a story that, unbeknownst to him, was later corroborated in a senior portrait prepared by his long-time friend). His essay made it very easy for me to empathize with him and also offered a quick psychological explanation as to why he had constructed such a seemingly macho façade.

At this point, you may wonder how reading this book and doing the Writing Discoveries it outlines will help you. First, it is my belief that achieving a greater sense of self-awareness will not only allow you to select the topic of your personal essay with greater ease, it will also enable you to delve into the most effective story about yourself. Second, the exercises in writing and reading that I provide are designed to reduce the unnecessary and often counterproductive stress you feel when facing a flashing cursor on the screen of a blank Word document. Last, after having read a number of actual college essays shown in various stages of development and supplemented with advice from your peers, you will write and revise your own college essay and short responses with a higher degree of confidence.

This book is not meant to be a mechanical, step-by-step advice column on how to patch together a personal essay. While you should expect to see guidance regarding the mechanics of writing an essay, the focus will always be on finding ways to reflect meaningfully on yourself as a person.

It is my sincere hope that you will feel calmer about the process as a result of the Writing Discoveries contained in this book, which were designed to throw a spotlight on your personality. Ultimately, my goal is for you to feel more satisfied regarding the fruits of your labor. I invite you to use this book the way I intended it to be used: as a guidebook of self-discovery through which you will end up composing just the right story about yourself in an appropriately engaging way.

Let the fun begin!

Writing Discovery 1

Self-Awareness

In some studies, social psychologists have shown what you have probably intuited all along: looking into a mirror makes you a lot more self-aware. Whether you begin your day by looking into a mirror to fix your hair, put on your makeup/refuse to put on your makeup, squeeze a pimple, or just to say, "hello, good looking!", it is unlikely that you also survey your face intently. Therefore, while the following activity may seem mundane, the purpose for doing it is quite different.

Look into a mirror for at least a minute. Scrutinize your face with care. Examine your facial features methodically. What are you seeing? What are your eyes focusing on? Start writing after the minute is up. Feel free to continue surveying your face periodically as you are writing. Describe everything you see.

Facial Features

1. Shape and color of eyes, length and texture of your eyebrows and eyelashes
2. Length, color, cut, texture of your hair
3. Color, consistency, smoothness, of your skin
4. Pimples, warts, blotches, or cuts
5. Length, size, thickness of lips
6. Facial hair or lack thereof

Writing Discovery 2
Negative vs. Positive

Reread the description of your face Writing Discovery 1. As you do so, circle every word with a negative connotation. For example, if you zeroed in on an unseemly wart with a tuft of red hair sticking out of it, you can surely circle that. (Thank you, Mr. Geoffrey Chaucer, for including this detail when describing the miller in *The Canterbury Tales*). The dried pimple or the chapped lips can also be circled.

When you have depressed yourself long enough, you can start lifting up your spirits. Underline every word or expression with a positive connotation. The intense brown eyes and the full brown, yellow or rosy cheeks are good candidates for underlining.

Count up each category and see which one of the two outnumbers the other. Reflect on your findings.

Some Questions to Consider

- Why do you think you have more negative words than positive ones or vice versa?
- In what ways does the way you see your physical face surprise you or not surprise you?
- How easy or difficult is it to focus on your face this way? Do you think others also see you this way?
- Do you think your face is ugly, beautiful, bland, or "too ethnic"? (Sadly, I've read this one quite often).

Writing Discovery 3

Changes

Find three pictures of yourself from different time periods in your life showing how some of your facial features have changed. The first picture should be from one to two years ago, the second one from three to four years ago and the third one from six to seven years ago. Take some notes about each picture. When you are finished providing an objective description of each picture, reflect on the way your physical appearance has changed over time.

Reflection Focus Questions

- How has your general physical appearance changed from picture to picture?
- How have your hairstyle and hair color changed? What has remained constant in its shape, length, or texture?
- How has your height or weight changed over time?
- What is the most drastic change you can identify on your face? (The appearance of facial hair, piercings, blemishes, clearing of skin are but a few possible changes one could mention).
- What has remained constant in your physical appearance in general, and, in particular, in the appearance of your face? The shape of one's eyes tends to remain constant unless one has undergone East Asian blepharoplasty (double eyelid surgery), which could be a story in and of itself. The thickness of eyelashes, though, could have been be increased with the addition of fake eyelashes and makeup or decreased as a result of an obsessive-compulsive impulse to tear them out.

Writing Discovery 4

Patterns

Read the descriptions of changes in your physical appearance in order to discern some patterns. Subjecting your past and present selves to your own critical gaze will allow your mind to retrieve some memories from the time period when the picture was taken. Write a reflection on these patterns of change.

Questions to Consider

- What made you decide to change your hairstyle (or for it to remain constant throughout the years)? If another person decided it for you, who was it?
- Who, if anyone other than yourself, influenced you to make changes in your clothing style, hairstyle, or any other feature of your physical appearance?
- How has puberty contributed to the changes in your physical features?
- What underlying needs prompted you to make a change?
- How satisfied or dissatisfied have you been with the change?
- How has the change affected the way others relate to you or how you relate to others?
- How different do you look now from how you looked six years ago?
- How different do you feel now about yourself, your place in the world, how others (family, friends, classmates, or strangers) see or treat you as compared to the time periods you have examined in the past couple of days? What has effected this change in your self-perception?

Writing Discovery 5
The Self Paragraph

During the last few days, you've spent an inordinate amount of time scrutinizing and writing about your physical features. Why do so, you may be wondering, if the admissions officers who read your application are not interested in your physical features at all? The answer, my friend, is right in front of your eyes. By looking at the exterior, you have invariably entered the interior. Much of your personality has been influenced by the way you have seen yourself. Moreover, your self-perceptions have changed in substantial ways since fifth grade, as is clear from the writing you have done up to this point.

Therefore, it is time for you to iron out a paragraph about your self. Reread Writing Discovery 1 and 2. Start your paragraph with a vivid and objective description of a physical feature in your appearance (for example, "I have a mole on the right side of my chin with two hairs sticking out of it"). Then make a number of evaluative statements about this feature ("I used to hate it," or "it never bothered me until...") and its impact on your self-perception ("It made me shy"). Of course, the above parenthetical sentences are extreme reductions. Develop each assertion in the logical progression that comprises your paragraph. Don't limit yourself to a paragraph if you find that a stream of long repressed memories suddenly floods your consciousness. We are still in the brainstorming phase; the more memories emerge, the better.

Writing Discovery 6

The Way I Am

Today, you will make use of all previous Writing Discoveries in order to compile a list of characteristics that describe you. The more nuanced and detailed this list is, the more useful it will be. For example, I could write that I am a self-assured yet quiet person who tends to observe social interactions more so than partake in them; I tend to make puns with the intent to reveal my acerbic wit—to make people like me better and think I'm smart—but this endeavor tends to backfire when a pun is not appreciated or totally misunderstood. You get the drift. This can go on and on.

If you end up free-writing page upon page of unfiltered and personal reflections on how you see yourself today as opposed to how you used to see yourself, you should feel overjoyed. Much of what you will have written now may become very useful raw material later as you endeavor to compose a coherent response about yourself in response to various essay questions.

In addition, you may even find this type of writing therapeutic. It may even lead to taking positive steps towards eliminating useless and often self-inflicted stress from your personal life. All kidding aside, if you need help getting to this point then your first steps should really take you to your guidance counselor or therapist.

Writing Discovery 7

In Three Phrases

Narrow down Writing Discovery Part 6 to three distinct descriptors that best reflect your personality. For example, "still hopelessly inhibited," "extremely perceptive," and "not easily angered or offended." Once you have three accurate descriptors, you are ready to brainstorm about the stories that best reflect these essential character traits about you.

1. _____

   _____

2. _____

   _____

3. _____

   _____

Personality Traits Word Bank

Petty, magnanimous, selfless, selfish, empathetic, self-absorbed, open-minded, sociable, introverted, extroverted, depressed, repressed, balanced, (not) easily frustrated/angered, vindictive, decisive, indecisive, independent, dependent, purposeful, orderly, principled, self-critical, stable, well-rounded, urbane, tractable, idiosyncratic, impressionable, glamorous, whimsical, stubborn, fatalistic, domineering, flamboyant, lazy, materialistic, spiritual, pugnacious, pretentious, quirky, strong-willed, self-indulgent, venal, unreliable, reliable, reflective, disciplined, eloquent, flexible, focused, discreet, humorous, idealistic…The list could go on and on, but I hope you get the idea.

Writing Discovery 8

Self-Image and Image for the College

You are now ready to work out just what image of yourself you'd like to convey to the college admissions officers. Clearly, even if you were to self-select some of the negative personality traits from yesterday's list as your first instinct, you really should not put these in the forefront as the most dominant traits of your personality. After all, who'd want to admit a *lazy, materialistic and easily-angered student* to an Ivy League or selective college? In contrast, you should construct an image of yourself as a young person who is aware of his or her maturation ("I used to be easily-angered, lazy, and materialistic but changed as a result of X, Y, or Z..."). If you are still "lazy," you will need to frame it in a more positive way.

Brainstorm about how you have changed or grown as a person in the last few years. If your self-image is still mostly negative, shift away from those traits and focus on the more positive aspects of your personality. Go ahead and expand on your positive, valuable, and sought-after characteristics. This is the image of yourself that you want your story to illustrate.

Writing Discovery 9

Recollection of Events, Places, People

Reread what you've written up to this point. When you are finished reading, set your timer to 60 seconds (or 90 seconds). Close your eyes and let your mind wander about anything you've just read until you hear the beep.

Welcome back! Now, settle upon a dominant image you want to convey about yourself. Let your mind retrieve some stories associated with that image. Begin writing down possible scenarios that involved growth you achieved as a result of conflict (external *and* internal) and include some kind of a resolution. Use a list form without adding many details. (For example, one may write, "the time I broke my wrist in seventh grade," "the death of my grandmother," "babysitting my younger brother," "when I left my flute on the subway," "my uncle from Florida and I," "the park where I run track and field").

1. _____

   _____

2. _____

   _____

3. _____

   _____

4. _____

   _____

5._____

_____

6._____

_____

7._____

_____

8._____

_____

9._____

_____

10._____

_____

Let the Fun Begin

Writing Story 1

Pick one of the possible story lines you identified yesterday. Don't worry much about details like form or which essay prompt your story line addresses. Rather, delve into the details of the story as much as you can. At this point, what matters is how much you can remember about the event(s) and your reactions to them.

Remember: we are all a part of various social networks and make sense of our experiences based on our position within each network. This piece should be as long as it takes for all the details, people and feelings to emerge. If you have emails or chats associated with the event you are about to describe, reread them first before you begin writing. You never know what can spur your recollections further.

Let the Fun Continue

Writing Story 2

Pick another story line from Writing Discovery 9 and write in detail about it. This time, try to find some pictures that are associated with the event. Again, the purpose of the pictures is to enable you to retrieve detailed memories.

Let the Fun Continue

Writing Story 3

Pick yet another story from Writing Discovery 9 and write out the story in detail. Today, you will make use of scents, smells or tastes associated with the story. For example, if you know you wore a particular type of perfume or used a certain kind of deodorant in your freshman year and still have access to this particular brand, get it out and smell it. If you recall that a particular type of food (chocolate, ice cream, fruit, or snack) was also involved in the episode, get your hands on the said type of food and taste it. This technique did wonders for the French writer, Marcel Proust. For him, the taste of a "petite madeleine" cake triggered a deluge of detailed, childhood memories that came to form seven volumes in his monumental novel, *Remembrance of Things Past*.

NOTE: If you'd like to write more than three stories that illustrate various aspects of your personality, please do so. It will *not* be a waste of time. The college applications you will be working on require numerous supplements. Much of what you manage to write at this point will become very valuable later. Just to give you a clue, a brief survey of the supplements found in applications used by a few colleges yielded the following questions:

- What are your favorite books? (50 words) [You can select the books that align with your personality in the best way]
- What newspapers, magazines, or websites do you enjoy? (50 words)
- Describe yourself in five words. [How great that you've already done this!]
- Who/what is a source of inspiration for you? (200 characters).
- Please tell us more about your cultural background and identity in the space below (100 word limit).

- We know you lead a busy life, full of activities, many of which are required of you. Tell us about something you do for the pleasure of it. (100 words or fewer).
- Tell us about the most significant challenge you've faced or something important that didn't go according to plan. How did you manage the situation? (200-250 words)

Practical Advice From Stuyvesant High School Graduates

Before we move on with writing, I'd like you to read a few pieces of advice. At this time, I'll let my former students do the talking since they have successfully completed the process you are only just beginning and can tell you what to look out for.

The foremost advice coming from your peers is really also the most obvious one: do not procrastinate. You will need a lot of time to create an effective college application. The process includes doing extensive online and other types of research about each college you wish to attend. Based on their own personal experiences, my students recommend that you begin working on the essay in August. Naturally, if you got your hands on this book in September or October (or even later), you really need to get to work at once.

So, what can you do to research colleges besides exploring websites?

> "Every weekend, holiday, and summer, I would sign up for as many college tours possible not only to show interest (important for liberal arts) but also to learn about the school myself."
> —Larissa Lam (Babson College, Class of 2021)

But which schools should you spend time on researching?

> "Have a **diverse** school list, and fall in love with several dream schools, not just one."
> —Karol Regula (Williams College, Class of 2021)

This means that your dream schools should not be limited to one type. A list consisting of Harvard, Yale, MIT, Princeton and a couple of safety schools is not sufficiently diverse. As Larissa suggests, do your research thoroughly and extensively, especially if it's clear that your GPA or extracurricular activities will not put you in the absolute top six per cent in the country. (Just to drive this statistic home, Harvard's admission rate for the Class of 2021 was around 6 per cent of all applicants). Let's see what else Larissa has to say on this topic.

> "As a mediocre student, in Stuy [or in any other specialized or selective high school], it may seem like no college out there will accept you. That's wrong. There *are* colleges out there that will accept you, but need to apply to the right ones. Be realistic about your choices. Ivies and other brand name schools are not the only schools out there. Don't waste time applying to schools that you know you won't be able to afford. There are other schools that provide a good education, good resources, and are willing to invest in every student. For brand name schools, unless you're dirt poor, you're going to be drowning in debt."

Larissa makes a very good point, especially when it comes to financial aid. It's very important for you to seek out advice and do your homework on finding the kinds of financial aid available to you at each school in which you are interested. I know the last thing you want to do right now is to wrap your mind around the financial obligations and costs associated with attending top, brand name schools; the thrill of the chase and the imagined glory of "making it" to your dream school at this point may still outweigh the somber realities of what happens if you actually do get in and receive little to no financial aid.

Just to remind you of how ridiculously expensive higher education has become, let me share some truly frightful facts with you based on information colleges published on their websites. In 2017-2018, tuition for the College of Arts and Sciences at New York University was $50,000 *per year* while living in a dorm cost another $9,000 to $21,000, depending on the room. This comes to a total of $236,000 for the cheapest option. In this same year, tuition at Yale University was $47,600 per year, not including room, board, or other fees. When you add all of those into the mix, you could end up paying $266,000 for a Bachelor's degree. Harvard College's tuition was $43,280 per year without room and board and $63,025 with it, adding up to $252,100 for four years. You get the point. Without tuition assistance or very rich parents, your dream school can very easily turn into a long-term financial nightmare.

Now, it is true that Harvard, for example, offers generous financial aid to students whose parents make less than $65,000 a year and have very little in terms of assets. In fact, if you fall into this category, Harvard will pick up the entire tab and you will not be asked to pay anything.[4] But it is essential that you do your homework and check what factors are involved when it comes to receiving financial aid at each and every one of the schools you are currently considering. The good news is that you are in a great position to do a Google search to find out what each school's tuition is and what financial aid they are advertising as a start.

You should only allow yourself to fall in love with a school after you and your parents/guardians have determined whether you can afford a particular college. I know this is a very tall order. After all, you have competing drives and interests. Whether it's originating from your parents or your peers, the pressure to get into the "best schools" is often rather intense. Of course, in the final analysis, the "best" school is the one that suits you the most, develops you as a scholar and offers a rigorous program that will prepare you for your selected career path.

As soon as you have an idea of where you *can* apply, avoid what Karol describes as having turned into a complete waste of his time. That is…

> "Applying to too many colleges. In hindsight, I should have written fewer, but better apps."

---

[4] See more here: https://college.harvard.edu/financial-aid/how-aid-works/fact-sheet

Indeed, quality over quantity is always preferable. As you compile a short list of schools, keep the criteria mentioned above in mind while also making sure to include a variety of school types.

By now, you have written a lot about yourself and are almost ready to write the first draft of your college essay. Let's see what further advice my students can provide for relieving some of the stress you may already be feeling.

> "Don't be scared to scrap and start all over."
> —Andrew Tang (Rensselaer Polytechnic Institute,
> Class of 2017)
> "It's perfectly okay to SCRAP your essay entirely."
> —Jennifer Yu (Cornell University, Class of 2021)

It is not productive to stress over what you are about to write in the next few days. In the end, you may decide to scrap it and write something completely different. You are the boss. You know best whether or not the essay draft you have produced is the best to submit. Even if you end up scrapping it, don't think that the time spent on creating your first draft was a waste. Why not?

> "When I was writing my essays, I found it helpful just to write a lot at first and then later mold what I had written into responses to specific questions. Different schools often ask slightly different variants of similar questions, but also often have their own unique questions, so I found this helpful."
> —Vandana Agarwala (California Institute of Technology,
> 2021)

When you write your essay, provide only those events and details that serve to highlight something about you as a person. Avoid jargon and too many details.

> "It matters less what the essay is about than *whom* the essay is about. I focused too much on the specifics of [soccer] refereeing [and not enough] on how much it mattered to me. If you're writing an essay about an achievement, activity—or really anything—focus less on what said topic entails and more on how it's affected you/why it's so important."
> —Laszlo Sandler (University of Chicago, 2021)

Laszlo's observation is supported by a high-ranking administrator from a very selective Ivy League school who does not want her name, title, or school to be identified lest you, the reader, construe it as an endorsement of this book. (Fine. Be like that!) Still, this admissions official's advice is so valuable that I include it here for you in its gloriously anonymous form (exactly the way she permitted me to include it).

> "Students should focus more on writing about a topic they actually know and care about as opposed to what they think a college admissions official might want. While there are certain themes/genres about which many students write, that fact alone does not render the essay 'trite' since each student will have a different writing style and have his work informed by his own experiences."
> —From the Admissions Office of an Ivy League school.

This should be quite reassuring to you. The above advice gives you permission to write about any topic whatsoever. No, you don't need to go out of your way to write about the most exotic trip, the most unusual experience, or the most extreme situations in the hope that this will make you stand out. Generally speaking, "exotic" trips or unusual situations do not let the admissions people see you in your natural habitat. Therefore, these types of stories are not very useful for admissions officers who'd much rather see a sample of how you behave or think on a daily basis. It should not come as a surprise that the most effective essays describe very mundane or even trite situations for the most part. The difference, though, is in the way the essayist inserts herself or himself into the situation involving a boring subway ride reading Kant, cooking dinner using grandma's old recipes, or even getting from one classroom to the next in four minutes.

The main purpose of writing so much in the last few days has been to give you a number of ways to see yourself while presenting you the opportunity to ponder just how you wish to represent yourself in the college essay and the many supplements the application requires of you.

> "Figure out what type of person your essay should represent. There is no predefined 'you' to write about. Especially considering the stressful timing, it's more efficient and effective to write as someone you hope to represent. This doesn't mean not to be authentic; just list certain traits you think you have and write to showcase them, rather than you as a whole person."
> —Jannie Li (Cornell University, Class of 2021)

Jannie is definitely correct: you will not be able to represent yourself "as a whole person." If you set *that* as your goal, you will be chasing an ever-shifting cloud in the sky. There is simply much more to our personalities than meets the eye. Knowing the limitations of this essay should calm you and reduce your anxiety. Already, you have produced a very useful list of personality traits and a number of well-defined recollections that you will make good use of in your drafts.

> "Start writing, even if it's terrible. Seek out advice from as many people as possible and weigh it heavily—any criticism they have might mirror that of your admissions officer. Write, write, write, and read, read, read; it's the only way to get better."
> —Alex Guo (Cornell University, Class of 2021)

Alex is absolutely correct: as in anything else, the only way to improve a skill is by actively practicing it while observing how others do it. Now that you have a firm direction, you can also keep in mind the next piece of advice that echoes what my poetry professor, the great Beat poet Allen Ginsberg, once shared in class: "first thought, best thought." (Of course, what he did not say but only showed in class is the thorough revision process that shaped his "first thought" into polished verse).

> "It's important to understand what you want to accomplish through your essay before starting. Your first instincts are always the best."
> —Courtney Chiu (Cooper Union, Class of 2021)

Don't worry about how polished your first draft will look. Judging by experience, I know that your first draft will be your worst draft. That's simply the nature of the game. While Alex is right in counseling you to seek out as many readers as you can for your drafts, you should also take into account what Namra and Jennifer have to say.

> "If you don't like a friend's edits, don't take them. Make sure to maintain your original voice throughout."
> —Namra Zulfiqar (Yale University, Class of 2021)

> "After reading it a lot, it's going to sound fake but don't stress about it too much."
> —Jennifer Yu (Cornell University, Class of 2021)

You have a distinct voice. Let it reverberate throughout the essay. You are now almost ready to read the Common Application essay prompts below. After you do so, you will see a number of final drafts that were submitted by my former students. Why?

"In order to represent yourself in a meaningful way to a college that likely sees applications from hundreds/thousands of students who all look very similar on paper, your college essays need to be really personalized. Your writing should say something about you that couldn't be said about anyone else. It needs to show why you're unique and why you "deserve" a spot at a college more than some other student who did similar things during high school does. To me, the only purpose that reading past essays serves is to get ideas for the writing style, not the content."

—Vandana Agarwala (California Institute of Technology, Class of 2021)

It is in this spirit that I present to you three college essays. I'd like you to see how each student personalized his or her application in a way that retained his or her voice and made use of solid writing techniques. You know yourself. If you feel you'd be better served by reading these examples before writing your own, then do so. If, however, you suspect that the essays will only serve to discourage you or tie your hands in some way then do **not** read them before writing your own first draft. In that case, select a Common Application question (listed on the next page with some brief comments) and write your draft by making use of the work you have produced so far. Relax. Then write, write, write, as Alex has recommended.

Common Application Prompts
from 2017-2018 and Models

1. *Some students have a background, identity, interest, or talent that is so meaningful they believe their application would be incomplete without it. If this sounds like you, then please share your story. [No change]*

A Brief Comment

In this essay, you are given an opportunity to discuss one significant area in your life that has had a very strong hold on you as a person. The range of topics for this question is quite wide. The topic you settled upon should show dynamic tension or growth. Immigration/integration, illness/healing, the development of a talent (cooking, playing the an instrument, chess, etc.) are but a few areas this essay topic includes.

2. *The lessons we take from obstacles we encounter can be fundamental to later success. Recount a time when you faced a challenge, setback, or failure. How did it affect you, and what did you learn from the experience? [Revised]*

A Brief Comment

Be clear in describing the obstacle or the challenge. Show just how or why it was an obstacle. Then, include your thought process, your real-time feelings in transcending this obstacle as well as the challenges, setbacks, or failures it involved. If you have to think very hard concerning what challenge or obstacle to write about, the chances are pretty high that it was not a significant enough event in your life. The lesson you learned in overcoming the challenge should be transferable to other areas of your life.

3. Reflect on a time when you questioned or challenged a belief or idea. What prompted your thinking? What was the outcome? [Revised]

A Brief Comment

To a certain extent, this question lends itself toward creating a more intellectual essay. First, you need to be able to set the intellectual atmosphere in which you grew up. This will form the basis of your received beliefs or ideas. Then, you have to identify a factor or emerging circumstance that has made you face an accepted belief or idea while also illustrating what change in your life had opened you to questioning this belief and how you ultimately handled it.

4. Describe a problem you've solved or a problem you'd like to solve. It can be an intellectual challenge, a research query, an ethical dilemma - anything that is of personal importance, no matter the scale. Explain its significance to you and what steps you took or could be taken to identify a solution. [No change]

A Brief Comment

This prompt is pretty self-evident. Here, as elsewhere, it is not the specific problem you focus on that is of interest (unless the topic you choose is the ethical equivalent of how to get away with murder). Rather, the focus of this essay should be your personal approach based on your personality and experiences in life.

5. Discuss an accomplishment, event, or realization that sparked a period of personal growth and a new understanding of yourself or others. [Revised]

A Brief Comment

All three parts of this question matter. The accomplishment, event, or realization should be described first, followed by a detailed account of the period of time when you changed your attitudes, feelings, or thoughts. It is important to include what was happening inside of you during this time and the tangible or palpable outcome to the internal changes you underwent in how you see yourself or the way you see others around you.

6. *Describe a topic, idea, or concept you find so engaging that it makes you lose all track of time. Why does it captivate you? What or who [sic] do you turn to when you want to learn more? [New]*

A Brief Comment

First, the last question should say "whom" not "who do you turn to..." But it's okay. You'll still get into your dream school if you use the accusative from instead of the dative. Be careful to provide just enough details about the topic, idea, or concept to make it understandable on a basic level to the reader without going overboard. After all, what matters is not this part but why it has taken such a hold on you. If you can describe why String Theory, Black Lives Matter, the American system of checks-and-balances, or ideas about reforming the NYC transit system etc. interests you in particular, you will have done a good job.

7. *Share an essay on any topic of your choice. It can be one you've already written, one that responds to a different prompt, or one of your own design. [New]*

A Brief Comment

This prompt is wide open for you to respond to in ways that the other six prompts do not let you. Yet, it is crucial for you to remember that your focus should always be on portraying your own interior life in response to your actual environment. Importing a past essay that you have written for an English or a Social Studies teacher will only work if the assignment had in mind the kind of showcasing of your personality in action the college essay questions are meant to elicit. Whatever you do, make sure that both the form and the content are in line with the six other essay questions. While I love poetry, I cannot image a very positive response from the overworked admissions officers trying to decipher an elaborate poem about your trip to Ohio in the few minutes they have for reading each essay. Can you?

(http://www.commonapp.org/whats-appening/application-updates/
common-application-announces-2017-2018-essay-prompts)

College Essay Final Drafts

In 1953, the British psychologist, Donald Winnicott (1896-1971), proposed the idea of "the good-enough mother." We tend to think the perfect mother is the one who caters to the child's every need. According to Winnicott, a mother who stops catering to her baby's every need as time goes by is "good-enough." In fact, the delay in response allows the baby to see him or herself as a separate entity from the mother. The "perfect" mother, on the other hand, does not allow for this development to take place. So, the "good-enough" mother is actually the perfect mother in that she is perfect in providing room for the baby to develop essential life skills.

Similarly, the "good-enough" college essay is not a "perfect" essay in the sense that it is devoid of all grammatical errors or always uses the right punctuation marks. If your essay ends up being completely free of any possibility of criticism then…wait, such an essay cannot possibly exist. If you think you need to write "the perfect" essay, you will only end up stressing yourself. Submitting an essay that is completely free of errors and sounds sophisticated beyond your age will only lead to suspicions. A "good-enough" essay, on the other hand, is a wonderful reflection of a significant aspect of your personality in action, one that showcases your strengths as a writer, a thinker, and a dynamic human being. A "good-enough" essay, pragmatically speaking, is one that does not slam the admissions door shut in your face with a subpar, poorly-written, loosely-organized, or rambling response but rather gains the interest or the sympathy of the admissions officer to the extent that s/he admits you to the school.

It is in the spirit of showing you "good-enough" essays that I present to you the following three essays (with much appreciation to the students who gave me their permission to include them here). Obviously, you may find some things to critique in each one. Nonetheless, you will also recognize why they were "good-enough" to prop the doors open to wonderful universities. The first time around, read each one without any assigned task. After you read the essay for the second time, fill out the questionnaire that follows each essay.

Princeton University Application Essay

Prompt: Tell us about a person who has influenced you in a significant way.

My middle school modern dance teacher, Mrs. Alleva, was never one to be caught up in the technicalities of dance. Her colorful spirit possessed an energy that couldn't be tamed by restrictive classical technique. Although every day in the studio exposed me to her unique limitless freedom, I've only recently learned to apply that same philosophy in my own life.

Mrs. Alleva often reminded us that the essence of our creative process laid in trusting our innate choreographic abilities while we explored the space around us. As she pushed me to improvise, to open myself to the vast realm of movement, I adopted her carte-blanche mindset. I placed less emphasis on the pointe of my foot and the extension of my legs, letting my body cautiously roam through my kinesphere instead. Once I trusted myself to ignore momentary technicalities, the quality and execution of my movements improved; it was almost paradoxical.

On the last day of middle school, Mrs. Alleva handed me a note. I still recall the last sentence of that letter: "And remember - sometimes, freedom is all that matters." After I spent three years embracing freedom through my work and in the studio, Mrs. Alleva still felt the need to remind me of its importance — and rightfully so. Just two years later, I found myself forgetting those exact words. I caved into the fast paced environment of my high school, planning and perfecting at every opportunity. I sacrificed the free mind Mrs. Alleva had so ardently instilled in me to become as efficient a student as possible.

During my sophomore year, my constant focus on precision consistently failed me at gymnastics meets. I messed up each one of my floor routines in one way or another; sometimes I tripped, other times I stepped out of bounds. The biggest challenge of my floor routine, however, was the daunting final pass. At each competition, I'd pause before the pass to ask myself the same questions. At what angle do I turn? How laid out should I be? Where do I spot? I was certain that with meticulous planning, nothing could go wrong. Yet every time, I fell.

It wasn't until city team finals later that year when I realized the value of Mrs. Alleva's words. While running one of my passes during warm ups, I landed on my ankle and twisted it. I spent the next two hours painstakingly planning out my course of action.

When it was finally my turn, I took a breath, wiped my sweaty palms along my shorts, and saluted the judge with an anxious smile. With every move, the final run crept up on me, but this time, I didn't take my usual mental pause. My mind a blank slate, I sprinted through the pain and into the last pass, leaping backwards into the air for my tuck.

My feet struck the mat and I stood tall. The universe, in its unpredictable nature, had found a way to remind me that all I needed was to free my mind. Without noticing, I did exactly what Mrs. Alleva would've wanted me to do: trust that my abilities would transcend every calculation I tried to make. I realized that after months of training and working on my technique, all I needed was to get rid of my doubts and exist in the moment.

Every year, I visit Mrs. Alleva and improvise for her classes. When I'm in the studio, dancing to songs on her iPod, I'm reminded of the free spirit that was born there. Even now, I occasionally overthink the solution to a problem or try to control my future, abandoning the faith I know I have in myself. In times like these, however, I channel the dancer Mrs. Alleva inspired a few years back and recall the letter she wrote to me. I remember that sometimes, "freedom is all that matters."

—Enver Ramadani (647 words) Princeton University,
Class of 2021

For this essay, I'll provide my own answers to the questionnaire. In the dominant qualities section, be sure to identify at least one contrasting characteristic. Your essay will be much better if you work some contradictory impulses, thoughts, feelings, or personality attributes into the story.

Dominant Quality 1: Desire for Perfection
Dominant Quality 2: Unrestricted Playfulness
Dominant Quality 3: Reflective self-discipline

Impressive Writing Techniques

1. <u>Concise, declarative topic sentences with appositives.</u> ("My middle school modern dance teacher, Mrs. Alleva, was never one to be caught up in the technicalities of dance.")
2. <u>A phrase repeated, gaining a different meaning</u> ("Freedom is all that matters.")
3. <u>Zooming in on the particular to demonstrate something universal</u> ("My feet struck the mat and I stood tall. The universe, in its unpredictable nature, had found a way to remind me that all I needed was to free my mind.")

Conflicts: Individuality vs. established norms, freedom vs. bondage, spontaneity vs. rigid forms, self vs. others, instinct vs. learned forms, automatic movement vs. cognitive control, emotional affect vs. cognition (that is, emotion vs. thinking), self-realization vs. social expectations

Resolution: Through outside encouragement and focused practice, Enver discovers that his internal voice or instinct often aligns with external conceptions. When it does not, loosening the binds of self-imposed expectations leads to more satisfactory outcomes.

Enver is cool and is suitable for our school because...

1. He is versatile. Not only is he a thinker, but also a dancer—and a good one at that. ☺
2. He expresses himself clearly (both verbally and physically, in dance).
3. He is aware of his weaknesses and is not afraid to point them out.
4. He is persistent, complex, and has a strong drive to succeed.

Common Application Essay 2

Prompt: Some students have a background, identity, interest, or talent that is so meaningful they believe their application would be incomplete without it. If this sounds like you, then please share your story.

v2.0 "10/25/2011, VA." I signed my initials and the date at the top of the wall and poked my head out from the tunnel. Looking down, I saw my coach and friends looking up at me. After countless failed attempts, I had finally scaled one of the most difficult rock walls at the YMCA in State College, Pennsylvania.

When I first began rock climbing in fifth grade, it seemed like I might never succeed. I watched in awe as people magically reached the ceiling, as Spider-Man might. There were walls that were slanted inwards, walls with concave handholds, and walls where you could use only rocks marked by a certain color of duct tape. But I soon found a coach to guide me, and even got my best friend to start climbing too. Climbing quickly grew from being just an activity to try out at the YMCA with my new membership to a much anticipated weekly reward. I grew accustomed to putting on a harness, strapping on my chalk bag, and squeezing into my shoes to try again to reach the top of a wall that had stumped me before. My friend and I even made our own route, marked it with bits of golden tape, and dubbed it "The Golden Girls". In eighth grade, when I became a volunteer, I enjoyed helping others start a new hobby, and also found that my own skills improved through coaching. Encouraged by this experience, in 9th grade I returned to help coach my middle school Math Counts team during afterschool practices. It was an activity I loved, and I only later realized how much I learned by being a mentor.

Climbing also taught me that working hard in one area can have unforeseen benefits in others. I've played soccer since I was five, and progressed to the school and travel teams in middle school. But although I had "a soccer player's build" (so I've been told), I initially lacked stamina and spent more time on the bench. Disheartened yet determined, I worked to build my endurance through running crosscountry in the spring, and continued getting stronger through climbing. I made the Stuyvesant varsity soccer team in 10th grade, and am now a starter and team cocaptain, which I could not have imagined five years ago.

"CS 3134, VA." Earlier this summer, I signed my initials to enroll in a Columbia University computer science class in data structures, CS 3134. I remember taking my first computer science MOOC (massively open online course) in seventh grade, when taking a university course online felt a far climb from where I was. I didn't finish my first MOOC, or even the second. But, like climbing, I gradually learned to stick with the classes, no matter how hard they got. I remember feeling a thrill every time my code worked as intended, or I was able to make it more efficient. Writing programs to perform functions that could be applied to problems around me was new and exciting, and strengthened my early interest in computer science. I completed several MOOCs during high school, which prepared me to take advanced math and computer science classes at Stuyvesant, serve as president of the Competitive Computing Club at Stuy, and build the confidence to pursue this interest further in college.

Whether in the classroom, on the soccer field, or in the climbing gym, persistence in the face of prior difficulty is something that I've come to really value. Looking ahead, I hope to keep this lesson close as I embark on channeling my skills towards doing good for the communities around me. In college and beyond, I hope to apply my training to hard challenges in technology, medicine, energy, and other fields. And I will remember the empowering feeling that hard work pays off, especially when you're doing something you love.

Vandana Agarwala (Word Count: 641)

Dominant Quality 1: _____

Dominant Quality 2: _____

Dominant Quality 3: _____

Impressive Writing Techniques

1. _____

2. _____

3. _____

Conflicts: _____

Resolution: _____

Vandana is cool and is suitable for our school because...

1. _____

2. _____

3. _____

4. _____

Common App Long Essay 3

Prompt: Some students have a background, identity, interest, or talent that is so meaningful they believe their application would be incomplete without it. If this sounds like you, then please share your story.

I can't recall ever hating a character more than I hated the hyphen. Seemingly innocent, it's a small line not low enough to be an underscore, not long enough to be a dash, villainous in its own right.

In my life, its primary purpose is to both compound and separate Muslim and American. I consider them equally important yet separate parts of me. But to many, I cannot be one without the other. It doesn't matter that I grew up in Brooklyn playing ball and freeze-tag in the streets; to some, my brown skin shouts foreigner in my own country. It doesn't matter that I wake up at five to pray; my uncovered hair screams heretic in my own religion.

For the longest time, my religion took the backseat to assimilation because I was afraid of discrimination. As a child, having faced Islamophobic slurs from both strangers and friends alike, I realized that I would be treated differently if I was Muslim. So, if someone asked why I was wearing long pants in August, I'd say I felt a little chilly. If someone asked why I didn't eat bacon, I'd say I didn't like the taste. I wasn't lying, just sidestepping the truth. I was hiding a part of myself to ensure that I wouldn't be an outsider, that others wouldn't feel uncomfortable around me. But every time I danced around the truth, I was failing both myself and my dance partners.

The summer before my junior year, I was faced with the tempting opportunity to waltz once again at a design program at North Carolina State University. Despite being one of three people of color there, I didn't feel out of place until one day at breakfast where one of my closest friends turned to me and assumingly asked, "What church do you attend?"

Two possible responses and outcomes raced through my mind:

1. I tell them I don't remember the name, and the conversation comfortably continues.

2. I explain to them that I'm Muslim, explain that it's not what the mainstream media makes it out to be, and possibly make them uncomfortable.

I chose the latter.

I saw the glimmer of confusion and fear I expected in their eyes, but after long conversations through breakfast, studio time, lunch, and karaoke, I felt less guilt and fear about the religion I had grown up with. I had been afraid that they would be afraid because of the distorted image of Islam they had been exposed to. But they were accepting and I realized that honest interactions lead to humanization.

I came back with a renewed appreciation for my religion, deciding that although being forthright could be unsafe, my Islamic faith and my American culture would both ride shotgun. Living between two ideologies that some perceive to be "at war," I can be the humanizing factor. I've become an ambassador of my religion, educating others through my unique perspective by helping tie it to the American culture I love so much. I combine Middle Eastern culture with the western appreciation of dance by directing a Belly Dance crew.

I try to remove the stigma that shrouds traditions such as henna tattoos by organizing volunteers to apply henna at local hospitals to encourage healing. I love designing and creating my own clothes because it allows me to maintain the modesty my faith encourages while incorporating western fashion trends.

Sometimes I'm tempted to revert to that first response because I know every situation won't work out as well as the first one did. I'm still afraid of what might happen if I begin to speak out. But I've realized that although blissful ignorance may be more comfortable, it's not the right way to live.

I suppose I'm a hyphen in my own way, helping to connect the two, but understanding the necessity of their separation.

Perhaps it isn't so bad after all.

—Namra Zulfiqar (Word Count: 650)

Dominant Quality 1: _____

Dominant Quality 2: _____

Dominant Quality 3: _____

Impressive Writing Techniques

1. _____

2. _____

3. _____

Conflicts: _____

Resolution: _____

Namra is cool and is suitable for our school because...

1. _____

2. _____

3. _____

4. _____

There are two ways to proceed:

1. First, fill out a questionnaire **for yourself** such as the ones you have just done for Vandana and Namra and then write your first draft.

2. First, write your essay draft and then fill out the questionnaire.

In either case, give your first draft and a blank questionnaire to somebody you trust. Ask him or her to fill it out based on the essay you wrote. When you get back the questionnaire, compare it to the one you filled out yourself. If the two are very different, you will know that your essay did not succeed in conveying exactly what you had intended it to do so.

This should be fun.

First Round of Revisions
with a Purpose

While visiting my classes, a former admissions officer once told my students to pay attention to grammar and spelling because, as she put it, "mistakes create a noise." It is certainly the case that most writers make mistakes in writing. I sure do. With a high-stakes writing piece such as the college essay, though, it is essential that you go over every single sentence with a fine-tooth comb in order to eliminate all the "noisy" errors. Obviously, it makes good sense to ask your English teacher, a trusted friend, a supportive parent, a staff member at the writing center (if your school has one), or anyone with strong writing skills (including peers) to take a careful look at your draft and offer meaningful feedback on it. The sooner you do this, the more time you'll have to consider any suggested revisions.

Spend the next week reading up on some of the more basic rules of sentence and paragraph formation. If brushing up more on a particular aspect of writing than on some of the others makes more sense to you, then go ahead and do so by all means. For now, leave your essay alone in order to gain some critical distance from it. In addition, a few days spent in the company of grammar rules will make it easier for you to spot the areas in your writing that most urgently need fixing. This not only applies to the college essay, but also to any piece of writing you may have to produce in the future.

Session 1

Tense Consistency

By far, shifts in verb tense tend to be one of the most common errors in high school essays. Make sure you use tenses consistently within a sentence. For example, if the first half of the sentence is in the Simple Present tense, the rest of it needs to be in Simple Present as well. It's not, "I do my homework as soon as I received it." (Find the error and correct it).

Know when you need to use Past Perfect ("I had been"), Present Perfect ("I have been"), and Simple Past ("I was"). Using the Simple Past, for instance, when you ought to use the Past Perfect in your college essay will not induce the college admissions officer to tear it up into dozens of tiny pieces and throw an immediate ticker tape parade over her desk while yelling "inadmissible, inadmissible!" Much more has to happen before s/he flips out. Still, using your tenses correctly adds another layer of sophistication to your voice and clarity to your narrative.

Thinking that it will lend a more immediate feel to their essay, some students make use of the Simple Present tense in the introductory paragraph. Here is an example: "I am about to enter the stage. The crowd is already clapping. When the curtains lift, I nervously take my seat on the bench in front of the piano." This may be a wonderful setup for an especially graphic or important scene charged with action. Far too often, though, the transition from the present to the past tense looks forced and unnatural. Therefore, your best bet is to keep your entire essay in the past tense when describing past events unless otherwise prompted by your writer's instinct.

Session 2

Sequence of Tenses and Conditionals

The English language is incredibly subtle when it comes to expressions of events in time. Just take a look at the timeline below.

Very Distant Past	Past	Present	Future
Happened First	Happened Second	Now	Later
Past Perfect	Simple Past /Present Perfect	Simple Present	Future Perfect
(had been)	(was/has been)	(is/am)	(will have been)

Events always occur in time. When describing a series of events, make sure to use verb tenses consistently. Follow the rules for the sequence of tenses. Let's imagine John told Jane to meet him in front of the school after classes. The correct way of writing this is as follows: "John told Jane that he **would** meet her after classes" and <u>not</u> "John told Jane that he **will** meet her after classes." Why not? Because the auxiliary verb "will" needs to be in the Simple Past tense since the first part of the sentence is also in the Simple Past tense. And the past tense of *will* is *would*. This rule applies to all tenses.

Correct the following sentences.

Example: The sentence, "Before I learned how to climb a rope, I repeatedly fell on my behind" should actually read, "I **had** repeatedly fallen on my behind."

1. He climbed a mountain before he went to school. [Hint: the earlier event should be in Past Perfect while the later event in the Simple Past tense].

2. He was happy he doesn't have to retake the test.
3. Every morning, she puts on her makeup and brushed her teeth.

Conditional Situations

If you want to express a hypothetical situation, as in one that is a conditional, you will need to be aware of whether or not the situation is in the past, present or future and use the appropriate conditional structure.

Past Conditional: Had he done his homework [or] if he had done his homework more diligently, he would have gotten an A+ on the test.
Present Conditional: If he did his homework more diligently, he would get an A+ on the test.
Future Conditional: If he were to [or] should he do his homework more diligently tomorrow, he would get an A+ on the test.

The most frequent type of error in conditional usage is when a person uses the Simple Past Tense in a conditional sentence in order to describe a conditional situation in the past. This is confusing because we very reasonably assume that a sentence in the past tense necessarily indicates events in the past. However, in the English language, this is not so. Conditionals or hypothetical situations in the present are expressed through the use of the Simple Past tense. Still, in spoken English, it's very common to hear a sentence like the following: "If he did his homework, he would have gotten an A+ on the test."

Why is this formulation incorrect? According to the second half of the sentence, the student has already gotten his test back. This means that he had already taken the test. So, it's clear that the end result has already come to fruition. If so, the action of the first half of the sentence preceded the second half. That is, the student had studied, or not studied enough, before he took the test. The correct tense to use for the first half of the sentence, therefore, is not the Simple Past Tense, but rather, the Past Perfect. Here is what the sentence should look like: "If he had done his homework, he would have gotten an A+ on the test."

Session 3

Pronouns, Subject-Verb, Sentence Structure, Phrases

If you attended elementary school in the United States, you most likely began learning all about pronouns in first grade. But whoever can remember all those rules so many years later? After all, spoken English is much more lenient when it comes to pronoun rules than written English is.

An older attorney acquaintance of mine recently told me that even judges tend to misuse pronouns. How? In this way: "The defense should produce the witness that stated XYZ." What's wrong with this formulation? Well, simply put, demonstrative pronouns (e.g. that, this, those, these) identify nouns or describe objects, places or animals. For a human being, you always have to use a personal pronoun (who or whom). The judge should always say, "the witness *who...*" and not "the witness *that...*" Still, you should be comforted to know that you can become a judge, a doctor, a politician, a lawyer (or even a sloppy English teacher) who habitually misuses pronouns yet still keep your job! It's just that you should avoid making this error in formal writing, including your college essay.

Pronoun Antecedent Agreement/Pronoun Shifts

You will have a lot of personal nouns and pronouns in your essay. As you reread your draft, make sure that all nouns and pronouns are in agreement in each one of your sentences. If the subject of the sentence is in the singular, the pronoun should also be in the singular. If, however, the subject is in the plural, it needs to be followed by a plural noun. A frequent error in writing looks like this: "He's someone who knows their business." The word "their" is in the plural. What you need, instead, is the singular form, "his." What about this sentence? "I put my book bag carrying all of my books, notebooks, and pencils in their place on the floor." What's wrong? The antecedent noun is singular (book bag) so the pronoun used here should also be singular (its and not their).

Subject-Verb Agreement

While this rule, too, has been emphasized ever since you entered elementary school, you may be surprised to learn just how often students use the incorrect form. Therefore, a quick review of this type of rather "noisy" error can only help you avoid it.

If the subject is singular, the verb should be conjugated accordingly. For example, "Nancy and David goes to the movies" is obviously incorrect since the compound subject is plural and the verb here is singular. "The movies was good" is also not correct for the reason that "movies" is plural and "was" is singular. I suspect you may no longer speak or write this way. If you do, it's essential that you fix it; you do not want such a basic type of error to drown out your voice.

Types of Sentences

A sentence is a group of words containing a subject and a verb that adds up to a complete thought. This is also the definition of a Main Clause or Independent Clause. A Subordinate Clause or Dependent Clause also needs to contain a subject and a verb, but it cannot stand on its own because it's not a complete thought. Coordinate conjunctions (but, or, yet, so, for, and, nor—BOYSFAN) specify the relationship between two main clauses. Subordinate conjunctions (because, while, since, etc.) specify the relationship between the main clause and the subordinate one: "I cannot apply to Simian College because it does not exist." Notice that you could easily put a period after "Simian College" and still have a complete thought. That's the main clause in this complex sentence. The second half of the sentence is the subordinate clause. If you were to write that out on its own as "Because it does not exist," you'd get a sentence fragment since it cannot stand on its own: it's not a complete thought.

Sentence Types with Examples in Brackets

Simple Sentence: One Main Clause [John likes apples.]
Compound Sentence: Two or more Main Clauses [John likes apples, so he eats one a day.]
Complex Sentence: One Main Clause+One Subordinate Clause [John likes apples because they are tasty.]
Compound-Complex Sentence: Two or more Main Clauses+One or more Subordinate Clauses [John likes apples because they are tasty, so he eats one a day].

Phrases

Phrases do not contain a verb and cannot stand on their own because they do not express a complete thought. They are mainly used to modify the verb (as adverbial phrases) or the subject (as adjectival phrases). You may make use of a present participial phrase (i.e. <u>Getting up early in the morning</u>, I always…) in order to introduce the sentence by specifying the time period of the event it discusses. By the way, a modifying phrase that comes before the main clause is called an introductory phrase.

When you go over your first draft, pay attention to sentence variety. It gets very boring and repetitive to read, for instance, four simple sentences in a row—unless, of course, this repetition was meant to emphasize a point. See how you can either combine a string of simple sentences or separate a string of compound-complex sentences in your draft. In addition, make some of your sentences more compact by moving a detail from occupying its own sentence to becoming an introductory phrase. Let's see an example of this in action.

Namra writes: "Living between two ideologies that some perceive to be 'at war,' I can be the humanizing factor." Here, she offers two assertions: 1. She lives between two ideologies that some perceive to be at war and 2. She can be the humanizing factor [between the two]. Clearly, it makes good sense to combine these two assertions by turning assertion 1 into a present participial introductory phrase.

Vandana writes: "Encouraged by this experience, in 9th grade I returned to help coach my middle school Math Counts team during after-school practices." Here, she makes two assertions: 1. She was encouraged by an experience, which she details before this sentence. 2. She returned in 9th grade to help coach her middle school Math Counts team. This introductory adverbial phrase works well to explain why she had the courage to try being the coach of Math Counts in 9th grade.

A Quick Practice Run

Here is Enver's sentence in two main clauses: "I ran one of my passes during warm ups, and I landed on my ankle and twisted it." Rewrite it by reorganizing it into an introductory phrase and a main clause. After you are done revising it, you can flip back to the essay to see the original sentence Enver wrote.

Writing Effective Dialogues

While college essays often include dialogue, you don't *have* to write one if you determine that dialogue is an unnecessary distraction. As you can see, in the three samples provided, dialogue is very limited (if present at all). Still, if you decide to do so, your purposeful dialogues may position you more realistically within a network of human relationships and allow for greater reader engagement.

Dialogue Writing Guidelines

- Provide direct quotations only when the wording itself matters or it adds something substantial to your piece.
- Always avoid lengthy dialogues. Conversely, include only a brief dialogue.
- Punctuate your sentences correctly. Before the end quote, you should place a comma ("I really love you," she said.) or (She said, "I really love you.")
- Avoid adverbs in qualifying the way your characters said something unless this information is not given by the context. ("The funeral begins at 10:00," he said mournfully.) Of course, he said it mournfully! You don't need to write this! Now, if he felt joy, that's another matter. ("The funeral begins at 10:00," he said gleefully.)

Dialogue from Kyler Chase (Harvard University, Class of 2019): *I was doing homework when my mother called me into the kitchen. "Michaella passed away this morning. I'm so sorry." I stood there, ten thousand thoughts speeding through my mind, but I was unable to process any of them. I wanted to find something, anything to say. All that came out was, "I have work to do," and I quickly walked back to my room, slammed the door, and sat on the floor against my bed.*

First Round of Revisions

Basic Grammar and Structure

Having reviewed some grammar and writing issues, you are now ready to put all of this practice to good use. Open your first draft again—which, by the way, you should have saved as EssayDraft1 in order to make it easier for you to keep track of the changes you will be making. Print your draft out if it helps you spot errors better on paper. Go over the essay with the following checklist in mind and fix errors or revise sentences as needed. When you are done, save it as EssayDraft2.

Writing Errors Check List

- Word use or word choice errors.
- Sentence fragments ("Because I could").
- Run-ons and comma splices ("Don't forget to apply, if you do, you won't get into the military, you will stay out").
- Misplaced or dangling modifiers ("Running after him, the man was mauled by a wolf"). [Can you picture a man running after a wolf asking to be mauled by it?]
- Frequent use of Passive Voice vs. Active Voice constructs (The above example is in the Passive Voice that can be made right easily by putting it in to the Active Voice—"…the wolf mauled the man.")
- Errors in punctuation, spelling and capitalization. Spell check won't catch common homonym errors such as using *wear* instead of *where, there/they're* instead of *their, accept* in place of *except, effect* in place of *affect* or the stylistic error of overusing the word *off* (as in *first off*).

Writing Discovery 10

Object Description

Descriptive language is your best friend. People—and remember, admissions officers first and foremost are just that—need to see descriptive words that allow for the quick formation of mental images. In this Writing Discovery, you want to improve your descriptive skills by taking an object (preferably one mentioned in your first draft) and describing its appearance in detail. Think of the scene as a movie clip that begins with a long shot (from the distance) and zooms in to an extreme close-up. Don't forget that objects have properties like texture, color and size.

Object Description Challenge

Color: translucent, diaphanous, azure, verdant, mauve, bright/faint+ color name etc.

Texture: harsh, grating, sparse, malleable, rigid, steely etc.

Size: miniscule, diminutive, vast, gigantic, prodigious, exact size by inches etc.

Example: Atop of its slender gray trunk, the seven gently swaying, curvaceous branches were covered in prickly leaves. From dark, vibrant green indicating vigor to brownish brittle, the palm tree's leaves densely covered the branch.

Writing Discovery 11
Object Description Similes

Today, you will tinker with yesterday's object description by coming up with a great simile (i.e., a comparison of two unlike objects using "as" or "like"). Take another object or action to which you can compare your selected object. Generate a list of similarities between the two. If the object is made of wood, specify what type of wood. If you are comparing its smoothness to something else, use an expression (for example, "as smooth as a licked popsicle"). The ancient Greek poet, Homer, was an expert in providing detailed comparisons between unlike objects, actions, or mental states in order to convey something crucial about an unfamiliar object, action, or mental state. Extend one of your comparisons into an epic or Homeric simile. Not only will this writing discovery stir your creative juices, it will also allow for more precise recollection and description.

Example: *As an elephant lazily flaps its ears in the heat in order to swat away a persistent fly from its dry skin time and again until the exasperated beast vigorously shakes its head with the pesky insect returning in triumph, so did the densely covered branches of the gigantic palm tree sway in the stormy winds.*

Your college essay is not the best place for you to include such an elaborate, Homeric simile. Nevertheless, it's useful for you to practice how to write a descriptive passage that incorporates something of your own personal choices or creative views of the world. Your word choices and comparisons form subtle clues that help admissions officers discern how you process the world as well as your place in it. Besides, how epic is it that you can now actually write a Homeric simile?

Writing Discovery 12
The Image Punch

For your writing to deliver details with the kind of extra punch that pleases rather than injures, you will need to practice writing expressions that contain metaphoric, metonymic or symbolic language. Go back to the sample essay and circle the dominant images in each piece. Then, revisit your own draft to identify the dominant image you have worked into the essay. See how you can make this image work better as a physical/metaphoric representative of your essay's central idea. Offer your mini-analysis of it as you see this done here.

1. *Seemingly innocent, it's a small line not low enough to be an underscore, not long enough to be a dash, villainous in its own right.* The hyphen as a villain is a vivid image. The rest of Namra's essay develops this image with illustrations.
2. *My feet struck the mat and I stood tall.* "Standing tall" is an expression that could be read as a tiresome cliché or as an allusion to a line from Frank Sinatra's "My Way." Here, the image of Enver literally "standing tall," works because it carries over into the symbolic realm, illustrating an evolving philosophy in Enver's life.
3. *I watched in awe as people magically reached the ceiling, as Spider-Man* [sic] *might.* In this simile, Vandana illustrates, in a humorously concrete way, her efforts to go beyond her physical and mental limitations and become a technological Spider-Woman, a superhero.

Comparing, Improving Drafts

It is normal to feel somewhat discouraged after reading other people's final drafts. After all, they look so polished and well organized. It is easy to forget that this is not the way their first few drafts looked. In order to ease your worries, take a look at how Enver's essay evolved. The entire sequence of drafts his essay went through can be found in the Appendix.

It also bears repeating at this point that you are the absolute owner of your essay. If you don't like it, scrap it! You should avoid getting stuck on an essay you come to see as a subpar representative of your voice or personality. Don't become obsessed with fixing a lost cause. If lost, start from scratch and pick another story line with another dominant image. (Remember, you have a lot of material to choose from).

Draft 1	Draft 2	Draft 3	Draft 4
On the last day of middle school, as we exchanged hugs while crying, Ms. Alleva handed me a note. What stuck with me even more than her kind words was the	On the last day of middle school, as we exchanged hugs with tears streaming down our faces, Ms. Alleva handed me a note. What stuck out to me from the	On the last day of middle school, as we exchanged hugs with tears streaming down our faces, Mrs. Alleva handed me a note. I still recall the last sentence of that letter: "And remember - sometimes, freedom is all that matters." After I spent three years embracing freedom through my work and in the	On the last day of middle school, Mrs. Alleva handed me a note. I still recall the last sentence of that letter: "And remember- sometimes, freedom is all that matters." After I spent three years embracing freedom through my work and in the studio, Mrs. Alleva still felt the need to remind me of its

very last sentence: "Escape the box - technique is bullshit, freedom is what counts."	letter was the very last sentence: "Remember, technique is bullshit, freedom is what counts." This principle defined my last three years in the studio and for some reason, Ms. Alleva had to remind me of it.	studio, Mrs. Alleva still felt the need to remind me of its importance — and rightfully so. However, just two years later, I found myself forgetting those exact words. I caved into the fast paced environment of my high school, planning and perfecting at every opportunity. I sacrificed the free mind Mrs. Alleva had so ardently instilled in me to become as efficient a student as possible.	importance — and rightfully so. Just two years later, I found myself forgetting those exact words. I caved into the fast paced environment of my high school, planning and perfecting at every opportunity. I sacrificed the free mind Mrs. Alleva had so ardently instilled in me to become as efficient a student as possible.

Notice how much longer drafts 3 and 4 become as Enver develops some points he merely hints at in his earlier drafts. Draft 2 contains a much longer quote from Ms. Alleva with the word "bullshit" smack in the middle. Why do you think the next draft is more effective without the line "technique is bullshit"? Are we being prudes here? My sense is that the self-portrait Enver constructs in this essay as a sensitive, technically-minded individual would not be served portraying Ms. Alleva as a person who dismisses technical know-how or meticulous practice. Clearly, Ms. Alleva did not mean to suggest that learning the techniques of classical ballet were useless. Rather, she tailored her message to fit Enver's needs as a contrast to his technically-minded efforts, which were beginning to eat away at his spontaneity and creative expression.

Revising Your Introduction

The introduction of your essay sets the scene and establishes the tone for the rest of the piece. It's also the first impression you make on the admissions officers. Compare the introductory paragraphs below. How do they set the tone in each case?

My middle school modern dance teacher, Mrs. Alleva, was never one to be caught up in the technicalities of dance. Her colorful spirit possessed an energy that couldn't be tamed by restrictive classical technique. Although every day in the studio exposed me to her unique limitless freedom, I've only recently learned to apply that same philosophy in my own life	*v2.0 "10/25/2011, VA." I signed my initials and the date at the top of the wall and poked my head out from the tunnel. Looking down, I saw my coach and friends looking up at me. After countless failed attempts, I had finally scaled one of the most difficult rock walls at the YMCA in State College, Pennsylvania.*	*I can't recall ever hating a character more than I hated the hyphen. Seemingly innocent, it's a small line not low enough to be an underscore, not long enough to be a dash, villainous in its own right.*

Apply your answers to your own introduction and then revise it accordingly.

- How does the writer set up the central situation, scene, or conflict?
- How does the introduction invite you to continue reading?
- In what ways is personality growth/change in ideas hinted at?

Revising Your Conclusion

The conclusion puts a final spin on what you've told the admissions officer about yourself. It enables her to see the extent to which the experiences you detailed in the essay have influenced your thinking and changed your behavior. Let's compare how Enver, Vandana and Namra displayed this type of development in their conclusions.

Every year, I visit Mrs. Alleva and improvise for her classes. When I'm in the studio, dancing to songs on her iPod, I'm reminded of the free spirit that was born there. Even now, I occasionally overthink the solution to a problem or try to control my future, abandoning the faith I know I have in myself. In times like these, however, I channel the dancer Mrs. Alleva inspired a few years back and recall the letter she wrote to me. I remember that sometimes, "freedom is all that matters."	*Whether in the classroom, on the soccer field, or in the climbing gym, persistence in the face of prior difficulty is something that I've come to really value. Looking ahead, I hope to keep this lesson close as I embark on channeling my skills towards doing good for the communities around me. In college and beyond, I hope to apply my training to hard challenges in technology, medicine, energy, and other fields. And I will remember the empowering feeling that hard work pays off, especially when you're doing something you love.*	*I suppose I'm a hyphen in my own way, helping to connect the two, but understanding the necessity of their separation. Perhaps it isn't so bad after all.*

Notice how the conclusion echoes the introduction. Revise your own conclusion.

Working on Supplements

Round 1

Since beginning this journey of self-discovery, you have produced what should be a very solid second draft of your essay. Now, it's time to take a break from it and let it sit a while. Show it to somebody you trust and elicit some feedback. If you get your essay back in a day, do not go back to it right away. You need some time to grow apart from it, so that when you read it again you will be able to read it with some critical distance. In the meantime, get started on the supplements. It will take as much time—if not longer—to compose effective short responses as it did to produce the essay.

Many of the supplement questions are intended to probe into your life even further. The experiences that led you to pursue a subject, choose your favorite book, influenced your reactions to intellectual issues, or defined your hobbies are all fair game when it comes to supplementary essay questions. While some are 200 characters short, others can be as long as 500 words. That's almost as much as the long essay itself. Luckily, you are ahead of the game since you've already written a great deal about yourself. In addition, many of the questions asked will not require deep introspection, but rather the simple recollection of extracurricular activities.

Naturally, the writing quality displayed in the supplements should match that of your long essay. For that to happen, you will need to devote just as much time to polishing your prose, diversifying your sentence structure, and making use of clear and concise words as you do for the long essay. Make use of the sections in this book on writing techniques and the checklists to spot and eliminate weaknesses in your writing.

Working on Supplements
Round 2

Prompt: Caltech students have long been known for their quirky sense of humor, whether it be through planning creative pranks, building elaborate party sets, or even the yearlong preparation that goes into our annual Ditch Day. Please describe an unusual way in which you have fun. (200 word max)

The Stuyvesant Math Team is a relatively small, tightknit community of students who, for the most part, are nerdy and academic. We enjoy going to math competitions together and devising solutions to math problems during daily math team practices. However, we also have fun together, often in unusual ways. After attending New York City Math Team practices at NYU on Fridays, we occasionally wander around the nearby Koreatown. Sometimes, we enjoy an hour at U2 Karaoke; I think singing, no matter how discordant or hysterical we may sound, is a great way to relax, unwind, and turn on a different side of our brains.

Karaoke, while perhaps an unusual pastime, has been a great bonding experience for several of us math team students. Watching two of my best friends recite every word to Billy Joel's We Didn't Start The Fire from memory, or standing up and belting out, "Who runs the world?! Girls!" karaoke has certainly provided me with ample opportunity to make fun of myself (and my friends) a little bit. But it has also brought us all closer together, made me less shy, and allowed me to grow into my own place at Stuyvesant.

A Few Notes on Tone

The above prompt invites applicants to show a less serious and more "human" side of their personalities. Here, Vandana manages to strike the right tone—no pun intended—as she describes her math team's favorite pastime, karaoke. Notice how she zooms in on a particular moment when the girls ask "Who runs the world?!" and answer "Girls." This comes across in a humorous, yet self-asserting way. It's especially clever because this way of thinking shows a healthy sense of self-esteem and affirmation of female empowerment in a field still dominated by males.

As in all responses to other prompts, the tone you strike is crucial. Formal but not stuffy, playful but not childish, self-confident but not arrogant: your tone of voice should make it easier for the admissions office to like you. Indeed, if you exude the wrong vibes, even an impressive array of accomplishments may do little to sway the college admissions officers to take your side. Banging on the door while shouting, "Here I am! Let me in! I deserve to be inside!" will do very little to endear you to the reader. After all, if other applicants possessing comparable accomplishments decide to knock on the figurative door more quietly while asking in a polite and likeable way to be let in, the applicant ready to break down the doors will make the gatekeeper's choice much easier.

If you know that your sense of humor falls outside the realm of social acceptability (say, you enjoyed setting cats' tails on fire as a child and still find that amusing), the college application is not the place to showcase it. While having a healthy sense of humor is generally appreciated, using a coarse or demeaning tone in your essay because you think it's funny will most likely end up costing you a spot in your dream college. How can you avoid this most unfortunate fate? Your safest bet is to elicit feedback on your long and short essays from various people, not only about the story, the grammar and the structure, but also about its tone of voice—which includes your sense of humor.

A Few Words on Content

Content is as important as tone. Admissions officers are especially sensitive to screening out potential troublemakers. High GPAs and wonderful extracurricular activities can be negated by a few ill-chosen words. Just recall Harvard's decision in 2017 to rescind at least ten acceptance offers based on memes and messages passed around a closed group of Facebook friends. [5] One of the lessons you should draw from this story and others like this, is that colleges are especially sensitive to screening out applicants who are seen as being intolerant.

Be genuine, forthright and honest in your essays. In the long essay—whether it is for the Common App or a school-specific question—develop a story that showcases a maturing of your sensibilities and sensitivities toward your social, school, or family situation within the context of a larger network of people. The supplements especially provide you with an opportunity to hone your answers to the questions by making use of specific experiences you've had mostly in your high school years.

---

[5]   http://www.thecrimson.com/article/2017/6/5/2021-offers-rescinded-memes/

Writing an Outline

Throughout the years, your English teachers have told you that writing an essay outline tends to make the task of writing the essay easier. For some students, writing an outline, comprised of a thesis, major assertions and intended examples, has become second nature. For others, the value or utility of outlines is questionable. While it's certainly the case that you can write any of your college application essays without resorting to an outline, it's my suggestion that you give it a try at least for the kinds of supplement questions that ask you to communicate your stance or opinion regarding a statement provided by the college. Doing so may facilitate the writing process a great deal.

Let's reverse-engineer an outline based on the response from Vandana's Caltech application. Read the prompt along with her answer. Then, identify how Vandana makes use of her past interactions as a predictor of sorts of future behavior.

Prompt: In an increasingly global and interdependent society, there is a need for diversity in thought, background, and experience in science, technology, engineering and mathematics. How do you see yourself contributing to the diversity of Caltech's community? (200 word max)

Growing up in State College, Pennsylvania (a university town) and now New York City for the past few years has exposed me to a world of diversity. My friends, of different ethnicities and with different interests, form a very diverse community, and have shaped my ambitions and dreams. NYC is a melting pot of cultures, languages, thinkers, and innovators. I live ten blocks from the United Nations headquarters, which often reminds me that we are members of a global community.

I believe diversity strengthens education. At Stuyvesant, my fellow students come from far-flung boroughs to receive education, and I greatly value their ideas in class. Similarly, I play in the All-City Concert Band with ~100 young musicians hailing from across NYC, bringing unique cultural perspec-

tives on music. I have also attended three summer mathematics programs in different parts of the country, with students from around the world, including Japan, China, and India. This gave me a glimpse into how education varies globally, and how this creates much-needed diversity in STEM problem-solving approaches.

These experiences have made me more prepared to innovate in diverse settings. I will contribute to Caltech's community by sharing my perspectives, and learning from those of others.

The Outline

I. Birth to Childhood: university town in Pennsylvania with diverse people.
II. Childhood to Teenage Years: New York City, living near the U.N.
III. "Diversity Strengthens Education":
   1. Stuyvesant HS's diverse student body.
   2. 100 musicians of NYC All-City Band from all over the city
   3. Three summer math programs: seeing how students from China, India, and Japan approach problems differently.

Because of its word count limitation, this response cannot be developed in much more detail unless you focus on one of these points to the exclusion of the other two.

Writing the Perfect Sentence

By now you have written a number of drafts. As a result, you have developed a pretty good sense of just what you'd like to convey about yourself. And while your essay as a whole needs to be "good-enough," it should include at least one so-called "branding sentence" that perfectly captures something about your situation. This perfect sentence should enable the admissions officer to recall your essay with ease in a conference or other type of decision-making situation. The most prominent place for this kind of a sentence is either at the very beginning or the very end of your essay.

Because of its importance, crafting and polishing your perfect sentence demands your full attention. Let's see how Kyler Chase arrived at his "perfect" sentence. Read the entire essay progression in the Appendix later.

Draft 1	Draft 2	Draft 3
When I was 15 years old, Michaella died. She wasn't my parent or my grandparent, and even if she was I don't know where she could have fit into my family.	An old hippie woman usually wearing a science fiction t-shirt, Michaella wasn't your usual babysitter.	An old hippie woman who spent the sixties on the back of a motorcycle with a copy of Lord of the Rings in her back pocket, Michaella wasn't your usual babysitter.

Kyler's task is to show how Michaella affected him in the long run. Notice how the introduction evolves from merely *talking about* her to *showing* her in action. The first sentence in Draft 1 gives away a major twist in the plot of the story too soon. The writer's thoughts jump from point A, inverting assumptions (i.e family matters more than outsiders) to point B, pointing out her absolute otherness in relation to the rest of Kyler's family.

In Draft 2, Kyler's sentence assumes a workable structure. First, he categorizes his babysitter as "An old hippie woman" (age and lifestyle). Then, he describes her physical appearance ("usually wearing a science fiction t-shirt"). All this is done in the introductory phrase before the main clause. Finally, Kyler evaluates her ("Michaella wasn't your usual babysitter"). While the description part needs to use details in order to turn into action and make the figure of Michaella come alive, Kyler is on the right track.

In Draft 3, Kyler provides a glimpse of a much younger Michaella, one "who spent the sixties on the back of a motorcycle with a copy of Lord of the Rings [sic] in her back pocket." This depiction purposefully highlights the former babysitter's two seemingly contradictory qualities: the action-oriented risk-taker (i.e., riding bikes in the 60s), and the voracious consumer of intellectually and emotionally stimulating works (i.e., reading *Lord of the Rings* four decades before it was popular). Thanks to the contrasting images Kyler employed in the first sentence of his essay, you can imagine how easy it was for the admissions officer at Harvard to picture Kyler as the creature of (seemingly) contradictory impulses: the tough football player who also plays the piano and sings with a big heart in memory of a hippie babysitter.

Go ahead and tinker with some of your sentences right now. Condense them into a perfect sentence. You will know it's perfect if it flows well and incorporates a combination of categorization, descriptive action (image), evaluation and characterization. Let your perfect sentence become your very own brand.

Farewell

We have reached the end of this book. In the last month or so you have looked into a mirror and seen not only the physical reflection cast by it, but also how you figuratively see yourself in it. You have identified your dominant personality traits and retrieved a number of significant stories from your memory bank in order to illustrate these traits. You have read three sample essays and seen what techniques work in the introduction, the body paragraphs and the conclusion of a "good-enough" essay. By this you have also come to realize that these samples really are good enough: they are not "perfect" essays. Now that you have reviewed some basic writing techniques, gone over grammatical rules and revised your drafts accordingly, you know that you, too, can write a good-enough college essay.

If you are still not finished and have more essays or supplements to write, make use of the steps in this book that helped you the most in producing your Common App essay. When your college application process is all completed, you will have become more mindful in observing and describing your environment and your mental life. No matter the outcome of your efforts, you should have a strong sense of satisfaction for the progress you have made. After all, there are many other factors at play when it comes to admissions. Just to give you a sense of the unexpected factors at play, according to an article by the behavior scientist, Uri Simonsohn, admissions officers' judgments can be influenced by (of all things) the weather. As Simonsohn's study discovered, on sunny days admissions decisions counted social and extracurricular activities more whereas academic achievement weighed more on days that happened to be overcast. [6]

So, when you have prepared your application, relax. You have done all you could. The rest is up to the admissions officers and the weather.

---

[6] Simonsohn, U. (2010). Weather to go to college. *The Economic Journal.* Published online July 17, 2009,
http://www3.interscience.wiley.com/journal/122515169/abstract?

Appendix

Read the following drafts. Pay attention to the way these drafts evolved into the final draft. As you read, consider the following questions. Feel free to mark up the text with your answers to the questions (unless this copy of the book belongs to your school or a library).

1. What aspects of the first draft are consistently retained throughout the revision process?
2. What disappears from the text? How does the elimination of the elements you have identified make the college essay stronger or weaker?
3. What literary techniques are used in this narrative?
4. What organizational changes can you identify from draft to draft?
5. What makes this essay emotionally engaging?
6. How does the applicant sneak in, as it were, some of his interests without necessarily sounding boastful?
7. Which part of this college essay is most effective? Why?
8. How does the introduction evolve? Which draft's introduction is the most effective? Why?
9. What do you want to emulate from this essay when it comes to writing your own?
10. What are some of your own observations about these drafts?

Enver Ramadani's Princeton University Application Draft Progression

Prompt: Tell us about a person who has influenced you in a significant way. (650 words max)

Draft 1

In middle school, I started to do modern dance. My teacher, Ms. Alleva, was brilliant to say the least. No, she wasn't some technical mastermind but what she had was more - a free spirit that couldn't be tamed and a limitless creativity. Our class was unlike most. Although we did spend weeks learning about modern dance's history, it's foundational techniques, and studying laban movement analysis, our works were defined by their rawness.

Ms. Alleva encouraged me to utilize my natural abilities. When we choreographed, we started off with improvisation - the most natural style of dancing. As we explored space, we picked phrases we liked and pieced them together to create choreography. It was this trust of natural instincts and risk that Ms. Alleva really ingrained into me.

On the last day of middle school, as we exchanged hugs while crying, Ms. Alleva handed me a note. What stuck with me even more than her kind words was the very last sentence: "Escape the box - technique is bullshit, freedom is what counts."

Flash forward to my sophomore year of high school and you see me forgetting this on the occasion. Despite my innate curiosity to discover and my love for creation, there are some things I just have to do through a technical lens. Gymnastics happens to be one of these things. It's odd because even though gymnastics is very much artistic, it relies heavily on perfected technique.

That year, I messed up in my floor routines in some way, shape, or form. I would fall out of handsprings and other times I would bail out of my pressed. My kryptonite, however: my last pass.

For the longest time, my back tuck (the final move in my last pass) and I were enemies. At what angle do I turn? How laid out should I be? Where

---

do I look? Every time I took a pause before my last pass I was certain I had everything drilled out in my head - nothing could possibly stop me. Until, of course, I fell every single time.

In late february, I was at the city team finals and was warming up for my floor routine. I was perfecting every single tuck and handspring on the long blue strip. While running one of my passes, I landed on my ankle and twisted it. I was in pain but that wasn't even the worst part - I had two hours ahead of me until I actually competed my floor routine. In fact, floor was our last event and not-so-fatefully, I was the last one to compete.

I spent the next two hours meticulously planning out my course of action on the floor. I asked myself the usual questions of how to rotate and where to spot except now there was the extra variable of how to not mess up my ankle more than I already had.

After a seemingly perennial wait, I was up. I took a breath, wiped my notoriously sweaty competition hands along my shorts and saluted with a smile. My first few passes were great; they never gave me too much trouble to begin with. Finally, my penultimate pass. I was headed towards the final run and there was nothing I could do to avoid it. Without taking my usual pause and breath, I turned around right after I was done and quickly ran for my next pass. With my mind a blank slate, I sprinted into my roundoff back handspring and leaped backwards into the air for my tuck.

For the first time in competition, I stuck it. Sure, it might've been a coincidence but the reality was that my best routine was a product of entirely accepting my fate. I didn't visualize or calculate. I wasn't focused on the technique. I just went for it.

Although at that competition, the mathematician in me wanted to damn the universe and its unpredictable ways, I have come to accept that sometimes, intrinsic abilities transcend calculation. Technique doesn't always equate to perfection, it just leads to overthinking. Sure, every now and then I'll catch myself trying with all my might to be precise and accurate in what I do; trying to find the answer to everything. In times like these, I channel my middle school self and remember that freedom is what counts. (717 words)

Draft 2

My middle school modern dance teacher, Ms. Alleva, wasn't some technical mastermind or a world class performer. What she had was more - a spirit that couldn't be tamed. That was the attribute she instilled into our classes. More importantly, it's the attribute I've come to appreciate more than anything else.

Our choreographic process always started with improvisational warm ups. The essence of the exercise was to explore space with a trust for our natural choreographic instincts and abilities. This free-spiritedness that Ms. Alleva encouraged allowed me to continuously open myself to the vast realm of choreographic possibilities. With every improvisation, I focused less on how to perfect my pointe or extend my legs and more on how to discover and explore. As I placed less emphasis on the technique of choreography, the quality and execution of my pieces got better; it seemed almost paradoxical.

On the last day of middle school, as we exchanged hugs with tears streaming down our faces, Ms. Alleva handed me a note. What stuck out to me from the letter was the very last sentence: "Remember, technique is bullshit, freedom is what counts." This principle defined my last three years in the studio and for some reason, Ms. Alleva had to remind me of it.

And rightfully so. Just two years later, I found myself forgetting those words more than I would have liked to admit. I grew accustomed to the fast paced environment of my high school, always planning ahead and being as efficient a student as possible.

During my sophomore year, my newly adopted mindset of precision consistently failed me in one thing in particular: gymnastics meets. That year, I managed to mess up each one of my floor routines in some way, shape, or form. Sometimes I would fall out of handsprings, and other times I would bail out of my presses. However, the kryptonite of my floor routine was the final pass.

The last move in my final pass, the back tuck, and I were enemies for a long time. I found myself taking a pause before the pass each time to ask myself the same questions. At what angle do I turn? How laid out should I be? Where do I look? Every time, I was certain that nothing could go wrong after my mental practice and calculations, yet every time, I fell.

Later that year, I was at the city team finals warming up for the competition. I was perfecting every single tuck and handspring on the strip. While practicing one of my passes, however, I landed on my ankle and twisted it. Not-so-fatefully, the floor exercise was our last event and I was the last to compete. Just my luck.

More so than the physical pain, I couldn't bare the long wait ahead of me. I spent the next two hours meticulously planning out my course of action on the floor. I asked myself the usual questions of how to rotate and where to spot except now there was the extra variable of how to not injure my ankle more than I already had.

After a seemingly perennial wait, I was up. I took a breath, wiped my notoriously sweaty competition hands along my shorts, and saluted with a smile. My first few passes were great. But before I knew it, I was headed towards the final run and there was nothing I could do to avoid it. Without taking my usual mental pause, I turned around right after I completed my penultimate pass and quickly ran for the final one. With my mind a blank slate, I sprinted through the pain and into my roundoff back handspring, leaping backwards into the air for my tuck.

For the first time in competition, I stuck it. Maybe it was a coincidence. Regardless, the reality was that my arguably best routine was a product of my full acceptance of fate. I didn't visualize or calculate. I wasn't focused on the technique. I just went for it. As a result, my natural abilities transcended all calculation.

Somehow, the universe had found a way to remind me of Ms. Alleva's words. In that moment and beyond, I had to accept that technique doesn't always lead to perfection.

Sometimes, I just overthink. Even now, I'll occasionally find myself searching for the answer to everything and trying to control the future. In times like these, I channel the dancer Ms. Alleva inspired in middle school and remember that sometimes, technique is bullshit and freedom is what counts. (753 words)

Draft 3

My middle school modern dance teacher, Mrs. Alleva, was never one to be caught up in the technicalities of dance. Her colorful spirit possessed an energy that couldn't be tamed by classical technique. But although every day in the studio exposed me to her unique limitless freedom, I've only recently learned to apply that same philosophy in my own life.

As dancers, Mrs. Alleva always reminded us that the essence of our creative process laid in trusting our own natural choreographic abilities as we explored the space around us. As she pushed me to improvise, to open myself to the vast realm of movement, I learned to adopt her carte-blanche mindset. I placed less emphasis on the pointe of my foot and the extension of my legs, letting my body roam through my kinesphere instead. Once I trusted myself to ignore technicalities, the quality and execution of my movements improved; it seemed almost paradoxical.

On the last day of middle school, as we exchanged hugs with tears streaming down our faces, Mrs. Alleva handed me a note. I still recall the last sentence of that letter: "And remember - sometimes, freedom is all that matters." After I spent three years embracing freedom through my work and in the studio, Mrs. Alleva still felt the need to remind me of its importance — and rightfully so. However, just two years later, I found myself forgetting those exact words. I caved into the fast paced environment of my high school, planning and perfecting at every opportunity. I sacrificed the free mind Mrs. Alleva had so ardently instilled in me to become as efficient a student as possible.

During my sophomore year, my constant focus on precision consistently failed me at gymnastics meets. I messed up each one of my floor routines in some way, shape, or form; sometimes I tripped, other times I stepped out of bounds. The kryptonite of my floor routine, however, was the daunting final pass. At each competition, I'd pause before the pass to ask myself the same questions. At what angle do I turn? How laid out should I be? Where do I spot? I was certain that with meticulous planning, nothing could go wrong. Yet every time, I fell.

It wasn't until later that year, during city team final, that I realized the value of Mrs. Alleva's words. While running one of my passes during warm ups, I landed on my ankle and twisted it. I spent the next two hours painstak-ingly planning out my course of action.

After a perennial wait, I was up. I took a breath, wiped my sweaty palms along my shorts, and saluted with an anxious smile. With every move, the final run crept up on me, but this time, I didn't take my usual mental pause. My mind a blank slate, I sprinted through the pain and into the last pass, leaping backwards into the air for my tuck.

For the first time in a long time, my feet struck the mat and I stood tall. The universe, in its unpredictable nature, had found a way to remind me that all I needed in that moment was to free my mind. Without noticing it, I did exactly what Mrs. Alleva would've wanted me to do: trust that my natural abilities would transcend all calculation. I realized that trying to perfect my technique doesn't always lead to my desired outcome.

Every year, I visit Mrs. Alleva and improvise for her classes. When I'm in the studio, dancing to a random song on her iPod, I'm reminded of the free spirit that was born there. Even now, I occasionally overthink the solution to a problem or try to control my future, abandoning the trust I know I have in myself. In times like these, however, I channel the dancer Mrs. Alleva inspired a few years back and recall the letter she wrote to me. I remember that sometimes, "freedom is all that matters." (660 words)

Draft 4 | Final Draft

My middle school modern dance teacher, Mrs. Alleva, was never one to be caught up in the technicalities of dance. Her colorful spirit possessed an energy that couldn't be tamed by restrictive classical technique. Although every day in the studio exposed me to her unique limitless freedom, I've only recently learned to apply that same philosophy in my own life.

Mrs. Alleva often reminded us that the essence of our creative process laid in trusting our innate choreographic abilities while we explored the space around us. As she pushed me to improvise, to open myself to the vast realm of movement, I adopted her carte-blanche mindset. I placed less emphasis on the pointe of my foot and the extension of my legs, letting my body cau-tiously roam through my kinesphere instead. Once I trusted myself to ignore momentary technicalities, the quality and execution of my movements improved; it was almost paradoxical.

On the last day of middle school, Mrs. Alleva handed me a note. I still recall the last sentence of that letter: "And remember - sometimes, freedom is all that matters." After I spent three years embracing freedom through my work and in the studio, Mrs. Alleva still felt the need to remind me of its importance — and rightfully so. Just two years later, I found myself forgetting those exact words. I caved into the fast paced environment of my high school, planning and perfecting at every opportunity. I sacrificed the free mind Mrs. Alleva had so ardently instilled in me to become as efficient a student as possible.

During my sophomore year, my constant focus on precision consistently failed me at gymnastics meets. I messed up each one of my floor routines in one way or another; sometimes I tripped, other times I stepped out of bounds. The biggest challenge of my floor routine, however, was the daunting final pass. At each competition, I'd pause before the pass to ask myself the same questions. At what angle do I turn? How laid out should I be? Where do I spot? I was certain that with meticulous planning, nothing could go wrong. Yet every time, I fell.

It wasn't until city team finals later that year when I realized the value of Mrs. Alleva's words. While running one of my passes during warm ups, I landed on my ankle and twisted it. I spent the next two hours painstakingly planning out my course of action.

When it was finally my turn, I took a breath, wiped my sweaty palms along my shorts, and saluted the judge with an anxious smile. With every move, the final run crept up on me, but this time, I didn't take my usual mental pause. My mind a blank slate, I sprinted through the pain and into the last pass, leaping backwards into the air for my tuck.

My feet struck the mat and I stood tall. The universe, in its unpredictable nature, had found a way to remind me that all I needed was to free my mind. Without noticing, I did exactly what Mrs. Alleva would've wanted me to do: trust that my abilities would transcend every calculation I tried to make. I realized that after months of training and working on my technique, all I needed was to get rid of my doubts and exist in the moment.

Every year, I visit Mrs. Alleva and improvise for her classes. When I'm in the studio, dancing to songs on her iPod, I'm reminded of the free spirit that was born there. Even now, I occasionally overthink the solution to a problem or try to control my future, abandoning the faith I know I have in myself. In times like these, however, I channel the dancer Mrs. Alleva inspired a few years back and recall the letter she wrote to me. I remember that sometimes, "freedom is all that matters." (647 words)

Three Drafts of the Common App Essay by Kyler Chase
(Harvard University, Class of 2019)

Draft 1

When I was 15 years old, Michaella died. She wasn't my parent or my grandparent, and even if she was I don't know where she could have fit into my family. But she was my babysitter, and probably the closest person to me that I have ever lost.

When I was in nursery school, most of my friends had parents who worked during the day and then would be home at night after school. Because both of my parents work in musical theatre, they were home while I was at school and at shows in the evening while I was home. For a while I went through a slew of babysitters. Most of them were immigrant islander women, as many babysitters are. But then there was Michaella. Out of all the babysitters you see in Riverside park on a Saturday afternoon, I don't know how often you find one that is an old hippie woman wearing a science fiction t-shirt, but that was Michaella.

When I was young, I was with her almost all the time. She would often pick me up from school and then take me to the park for a while. Michaella was a huge fan of sci fi and fantasy stories, and perhaps because of that so was I. While in the park, I would often come up with different games and stories in my head. I called them mind games. One day, created a game where I used the squares on the floor of the playground as a sort of playing board.

By the time I was in middle school, I no longer needed a babysitter like a had a few years before. I have a brother who is nearly five years younger than me, but when he needed a babysitter he had Jody, who was actually Michaella's daughter. But I hadn't stopped seeing Michaella. On the occasional weekend my parents would allow me to go to her house, sometimes to stay the night. In her house, the lights were always dim, there were bookshelves upon bookshelves cluttered with hundreds of different fantasy books. On a couple tables rested dusty ritual knives and charms. As you can imagine this was very different from my house, tends to be brightly lit and tidy. My parents are not particularly religious but they believe in going to Church here and there. And while my parents are not very big fans of games, particularly video games, I would play games for hours at Michaella's house.

One day I was sitting in my room doing homework when my mother called me into the other room. "I just talked to Jody," she said. "Michaella passed away this morning. I'm so sorry." I stood there for a second, ten thousand thoughts speeding through my mind but being unable to process any of them. I wanted to find something, anything to say. All I could come out with was "I have work to do," and I quickly walked back to my room, slammed the door, and sat on the floor against my bed.

At first I couldn't understand how she could have died so quickly. She told me she was getting better! When did she take such a turn for the worse? Because the last time I saw her... And then I thought about when that was. A month ago. A whole month. All of my grief and sadness immediately turned into anger and frustration. Not at the world, not even at whatever had ended her life, but at myself. All she had asked for was my company and I was too busy to see her for an entire month before she died. It was everything in my power that I could have done to help her and I failed.

For the first time in my life I felt that I had done some so wrong that the damage could not be undone. In the past if I had played badly in a game I could work harder for the next one, or if I had done something to anger my parents or a friend I could apologize and hope that they would forgive me. (692 Words)

Draft 2

An old hippie woman usually wearing a science fiction t-shirt, Michaella wasn't your usual babysitter. I couldn't compare her to anybody else I know. She took care of me when my parents were working until I was in middle school. When she was no longer babysitting me and only her daughter, Jody, came to babysit my little brother, I visited her house on the occasional weekend. For hours we would catch up, tell jokes, and play games. She would tell me stories from her life at my age and then give me advice about mine. She would always know exactly what to say if I was down. "Good grief!" she would say.

When I was entering high school, I started to see Michaella less than I had before. At the same time, she became sick. She had a tumor, but she assured me that the doctor was able to shrink it. When my mother asked if there was anything we could do to help, she asked only for my company. I came when I could, but it was still not as often as before.

One day I was sitting in my room doing homework when my mother called me into the other room. "I just talked to Jody," she said. "Michaella passed away this morning. I'm so sorry." I stood there for a second, ten thousand thoughts speeding through my mind but being unable to process any of them. I wanted to find something, anything to say. All I could come out with was "I have work to do," and I quickly walked back to my room, slammed the door, and sat on the floor against my bed.

At first I couldn't understand how she could have died so quickly. She told me she was getting better! When did she take such a turn for the worse? Because the last time I saw her... And then I thought about when that was. Over a month ago. A whole month. All of my grief and sadness immediately turned into anger and frustration. Not at the world, not even at whatever had ended her life, but at myself. All she had asked for was my company and I was too busy to see her for an entire month before she died. It was everything in my power that I could have done to help her and I failed.

For the first time in my life I felt that I had done some so wrong that the damage could not be undone. In the past if I had played badly in a game I could work harder for the next one, or if I had done something to anger my parents or a friend I could apologize and hope that they would forgive me.

Not this time. I couldn't go back in time and I couldn't apologize to her now. Soon after I decided the I wasn't helping anything and started to get ready to sleep. By the time my mom came to check on me I was already in bed, waiting to fall asleep so that I could have a break from my own frustration for at least a short while.

The next few days I found that my anger had reverted back to sadness, and the weight of regret rested on my shoulders. I avoided talking to anyone about it because I didn't know what to say. When Saturday came around I no longer had school to distract me. Alone in my house, I decided the best way to let it out was at the piano. After playing and singing happy songs for almost an hour, I decided to sing "Into the West," a funeral song from Lord of the Rings. When I reached the second chorus of the song, my eyes began to water and I choked on the words. I stopped playing because I could no longer continue. I looked into the mirror, and with tears running down my face and dripping from my cheeks, I noticed I was smiling. For perhaps the first time in days, I was really smiling. I don't think that at the time I could really understand why, but now later I realized that I knew she was off to a better place, and the one thing I could do to make up for how I felt I had failed her was to continue on to be the young man she said and believed I would be.

I had my chance to say my last goodbyes in a small service held later that month. I exchanged memories with the few other families present, but I found the best way to express myself was through music. I chose to sing "Imagine" by John Lennon, and when I left I was at peace. I resolved to always treasure every moment of anything I hold dear in life. I would sing every song like it was my last, and play every game of football as if I would never play again. I would never hold back, and thats how I could repay Michaella for all she gave me. Thats how I could become the young man she always said and believed I could be.

At the memorial service, I sang for Michaella. As I finished the song, I realized she would live on in me and the others present. Holding onto the wisdom and memories she gave me, I resolved to never hold back. I will sing every song like it is my last, go into every practice and every game like I will never play again. Because of Michaella I know to live life to the fullest and treasure every moment with those I hold dear.

As I traded memories and final words with the other families present,
I realized that her spirit would live on in all of us. As clichéd as that sounds
I believed it. I hold onto the wisdom and memories. (989 Words)

Final Draft

An old hippie woman who spent the sixties on the back of a motorcycle with
a copy of Lord of the Rings in her back pocket, Michaella wasn't your usual
babysitter. But she took care of me when my parents were working until I
was in middle school. Even then I would still visit her on the occasional week-
end. For hours we would catch up, tell jokes, and play games. She would tell
me stories about her life at my age and give me much needed advice about
mine. She always knew what to say. If I was ever down, "Good grief!" she
would exclaim, "This is just a little bump in the road."

    Once I entered high school, I saw Michaella less. A tumor was found,
but she assured me that her doctor could shrink it. When my mother asked
how we could help, she asked only for my company. I came when I could.

    I was doing homework when my mother called me into the kitchen.
"Michaella passed away this morning. I'm so sorry." I stood there, ten thou-
sand thoughts speeding through my mind, but I was unable to process any of
them. I wanted to find something, anything to say. All that came out was, "I
have work to do," and I quickly walked back to my room, slammed the door,
and sat on the floor against my bed.

    How did it happen so quickly? She told me she was getting better the
last time I saw her... And then I thought about when that was. Over a month
ago. A whole month. All of my grief and sadness immediately turned into
anger and frustration. Not at the world, but at myself. All she had asked for
was my company and I was too busy to visit her for an entire month.

    For the first time in my life I had done something so wrong that the
damage could not be undone. If I had played badly in a game I could work
harder for the next one, or if I had angered my parents I could apologize and
hope for their forgiveness. I couldn't go back in time; I couldn't apologize to
her now.

In the next few days, I avoided talking about it because I didn't know what to say. When Saturday finally came around I no longer had school to distract me. Alone in my house, the best way to let it out was at the piano. After playing and singing for almost an hour, I decided to sing "Into the West," a funeral song from Lord of the Rings. When I reached the second chorus, my eyes began to water and I choked on the words. I stopped playing, saw my reflection in the mirror above the piano, and with tears running down my face and dripping from my cheeks, I noticed I was smiling. For the first time in days, I was smiling. I realized that she was off to a better place. As cliche as that sounds, I believed it. And the one thing I could do to make up for how I had failed her was to continue on to be the young man she believed I would be.

In a small memorial service, I sang "Imagine" by John Lennon, for Michaella. I was at peace. Holding onto the time and wisdom she gave me, I resolved to live life to the fullest and to treasure every moment with those I hold dear in life. I would sing every song like it was my last, go into every practice and every game like I would never play again. I will never hold back and that is how I can repay Michaella. (621 Words)

About the Author

David Mandler earned his Bachelor's degree in English and French from Brooklyn College (1996) and subsequently completed the M.A./Ph.D. program in English and American Literature at New York University (2005). He has since authored a number of scholarly articles as well as a critically acclaimed book entitled *Arminius Vambéry and the British Empire: Between East and West* (2016), which has also appeared in Hungarian translation. His other published writings include articles in *The Budapest Times*, book reviews in *Hungarian Cultural Studies* and a short story called "The Loft" available on amazon.com. He plays the piano and loves to sing. For a decade, Dr. Mandler taught English literature and writing courses at Touro College. He taught at The Baccalaureate Schools for Global Education for three years before joining the English Department at Stuyvesant High School in 2010. Dr. Mandler has recently completed a collection of poems entitled *Circular Six* and a novel, *The Plunge*. He lives with his wife and two young children in Brooklyn, New York.

NOTES

Made in the USA
San Bernardino, CA
13 December 2017